OFWs MODERN DAY HEROES
Stories of Filipina OFWs

MAURICE HARVEY

Copyright @2021 by Maurice Harvey

All rights reserved. No part of this book may be reproduced in any form or by any electronic or mechanical means, including information storage and retrieval systems, without permission in writing from the publisher, except by reviewers, who may quote brief passages in a review.

This publication contains the opinions and ideas of its author. It is intended to provide helpful and informative material on the subjects addressed in the publication. The author and publisher specifically disclaim all responsibility for any liability, loss or risk, personal or otherwise, which is incurred as a consequence, directly or indirectly, of the use and application of any of the contents of this book.

WORKBOOK PRESS LLC
187 E Warm Springs Rd,
Suite B285, Las Vegas, NV 89119, USA

Website: https://workbookpress.com/
Hotline: 1-888-818-4856
Email: admin@workbookpress.com

Ordering Information:
Quantity sales. Special discounts are available on quantity purchases by corporations, associations, and others. For details, contact the publisher at the address above or you my send an email to the author at mauriceharvey35@gmail.com.

ISBN-13:   978-1-958176-13-9 (Paperback Version)
           978-1-958176-14-6 (Digital Version)

REV. DATE: 5.2.2022

ALSO BY MAURICE HARVEY

Shooting the Globe

Reading the Funny Bible and Other Stories

Into the Great Unknown

Light for Life

Blown up by the Bible

No Protocol for Me

DEDICATION

To Louie Bernardo and family.

FORWARD

Read this as an historical novel. It is based on true stories although names and places have been changed except where the individual has given permission. On the last page is a list of the people who told me their stories to whom I am deeply indebted.

A novel is a creation based on an author's knowledge, experience and imagination and this usually leaves the reader wondering which is what!

It is difficult to describe the immense contribution overseas Philippine workers are making to the benefit of the world. This novel is restricted to OFW – overseas Filipina workers, that is the women, although among the Filipino (men) there is another range of issues that could be addressed. No attempt has been made to describe fully, the improper conditions of work suffered by some people or quote the latest official statistics of OFW.

CHAPTER ONE

He lay down on his bed and began to wonder what he would do now. He had buried his wife two months ago after a horrific road accident. Now he was alone. How could he bear it?

After a few weeks of being alone, it wasn't getting any easier. The family had gone back to their respective jobs. They had rushed home on hearing of their mother's passing and had been kindness and love personified as they helped their father deal with the tragedy. But their lives had to go on, as did his.

Slowly an idea began to form in his mind. He had been thinking about a friend in Auckland who had a camper van, or what they called a motor home in the USA. After losing his wife, he travelled the length and breadth of the land enjoying the countryside and visiting friends. That's what he would do. Not travel New Zealand but America. He would go to the USA and hire a beautiful big luxurious motor home and tour the country. It would be a completely new experience and something that he had always wanted to do but his wife didn't like temporary accommodation of any kind.

He rolled off the bed and turned on the computer. He searched for an hour under 'luxurious motor homes USA.' There was such a variety and a 32-foot bus took his fancy. Sleeps four in luxury went the spiel. No special licence needed since he wouldn't be carrying paying passengers. Equipped with every modern convenience possible. That would do nicely.

Next move was to the travel agent and his timing was good. Seats available any day he chose. Within 10 days he was on an Air New Zealand flight to Los Angeles.

His flight arrived at 7.00 am and after checking into

a hotel near the airport, took a taxi to the motor home agent. It was a two-man operation, the owner and a man to prepare the vehicles for the road. He recognized him as a Filipino. 'How could you tell Sir that I am from the Philippines?'

'Oh, that was easy, I used to live there.' Then began a lively discussion about life in Manila. Alfredo, for that was his name, proudly showed him the special features of his 'bus.' This took thirty minutes and then he asked, 'Where do you intend to go sir, and when will your family come?'

'There is no family with me. My wife passed away three months ago and I am on my own.'

Alfredo looked at him carefully and thoughtfully, and said, 'Then perhaps you need some company. I think I can help.'

No thank you, that's the whole point of the trip. I want to be alone and enjoy the luxury that this thing that gives me lots of room and I can go where I want to.'

'But sir, please excuse me, but you need someone to take care of you. I think I can help.'

'No thanks, I don't need help.' Then paused and said, 'What kind of help are you thinking of?'

'Well, sir, my sister has just come from the Philippines, she came last week, and she could help you. She has lost her husband and is lonely and came here for a holiday. She could make your meals and cleaning and laundry sir; you would like that wouldn't you?'

He immediately thought of the wonderful young women who helped in the house when they were in Manila and Hong Kong. To have someone to care for him while on holiday sounded too good to be true. Servants in the home were part of their life for many years.

Umm, sounds good, but it was the last thing he thought

he would get here. Joe had spent his life travelling the world as an international photojournalist. This took him around the world numerous times. He couldn't even remember how many. He had studied many languages, three to public speaking level and a few at what he called market level. Otherwise, he relied on pocket phrase books. These had saved him many times, like asking for some soap in Russia. The floor lady brought him a towel. Then some toilet paper. 'Look here.' pointing to his phrase book. She squinted at it and said: 'Nyet. Nyet otspee.' He took that to mean glasses. Finally, after rubbing his hands over his body.

'Ahh massage. Oh, oh, Milo?'

'Nyet, I don't want a drink.' That puzzled her. He checked his small dictionary. Milo is soap.

Later, when she brought the soap she had a piece of paper in her hand and held it out saying 'podpis.' A quick check, oh that means signature! He often thought that he should have studied modern anthropology and linguistics. When he travelled he liked to try and identify people's ethnicity.

There was something about the people from the Philippines that had always interested him. They seemed to be everywhere. As the years went by they had become quite numerous. There were more and more of them. Over the years he had servants in the home - and with his family had lived in seven countries. It was the house servants from the Philippines that seemed to be the best. In most places you never hired a servant until he or she was checked out carefully and had good references. At various timed they had had Zambians, Nigerians, Fijians, Indonesians: some of these were excellent others not trustworthy. They never once checked on any of the four Filipinas they hired. That one applied for a job was sufficient. They never had to lock anything up like in Africa where there was even a lock on the fridge. They were faithful and reliable and could be left in charge of a house for weeks at a time. Like the time in Hong Kong when, after settling in a new maid from Manila, they left her in charge of the apartment after being with them for only two weeks. They were away for three months during which time there was no communication and on returning, everything was in perfect condition. And another thing, because he travelled away from home a great deal, it was important for his wife and children to feel safe with the house help.

'Let me bring her here to meet you, sir. I can call her right away: her name is Remy.'

'Tell you what, bring her to my hotel this evening and we can have dinner together and discuss it then.'

But the next thing was to decide which vehicle to hire. He wasn't sure what to call it as he explained to the owner, that it could be called a campervan at home, but here, what is it? I've heard them called trailers, caravans or motor homes. He was told that officially it is a motor home. But to Joe that sounded too permanent. He said he might simply call it his van or bus. There was a huge array from a tiny one bed with a couple the size of a bus for families of 6 or 8. The owner showed him the range and then sensing that Joe was after some real luxury showed him a huge bus considered to be the very best. 'It has everything for the man who wants everything,' said the owner. 'And you can have it for a very special price, even cheaper than some of the smaller ones. I am renting it out for a friend.' When Joe looked doubtful, he quickly added that it was fully insured and that there was no risk in taking it even though it wasn't on his stock list.

Feeling somewhat greedy, but with a feeling that it was time he spoiled himself, he agreed to take it, the price wasn't much more than a good motel room. He signed up for a month with the option of another two.

He lay down for a rest after lunch and thought about this sudden turn of events. The more he thought about it the more attractive it was to have a live-in maid to take care of him. That's how it was for years and years when they lived as a family in the tropics. The Filipinas were so good in the house. Yes, I'll take her provided I like her.

It was with no small measure of excitement that he waited in the foyer for Alfredo and his sister. I wonder if she is really his sister, not a cousin or an aunty. You could never tell with these people. The van was big enough even for some privacy away from her. Thirty-two feet long, gosh that's plenty.

Why am I down here he thought, long ago I learned to wait for the call in my room. I guess I am excited. Ten minutes later they appeared in the doorway. Alfredo was grinning from ear to ear and proudly presented the lady. 'Please meet my mother,' he said.

'Ahmm, pleased to meet you maam.' Then turning to Alfredo, he said, 'But I thought it was your sister who was coming.' But she reached out her hand and took his. 'Good evening sir.'

'Now, sir I have to explain, my sister could not come tonight, so my mother came instead. But don't worry sir, she will be here tomorrow.'

This is very clever; mother has come along to check me out before allowing her daughter to meet me. But that's quite reasonable and so typical.

'Do you have a name?'

'Yes of course, sir she's Renny.'

'I am pleased to meet you Renny.' Then after a moment, 'It's time to eat, come this way.'

He led them to the dining room his thinking being that would be better than the informal coffee shop. But his mind was in a whirl. What to do. He couldn't take on the daughter next morning without checking her out. Sure, he could learn a lot about her from the mother. There's only one thing to do. Go through the dinner tonight and meet daughter tomorrow and delay departure for a day. If she passed the test, then daughter could come tomorrow for dinner.

Renny proved to be a likable person and had come for a three-month holiday with her son. There was always the hope that he would sponsor her and daughter Remy to the USA at some time.

The evening passed quickly as he enjoyed the company of mother and son. They were both interesting people. Renny was quite a beautiful woman, slim and neat, whose forty-nine years he discovered were well hidden behind a wrinkle free face and clear black eyes. Maybe daughter was like her mother. In fact, he began to think that if daughter did not want to come or wasn't allowed to, then mother would do just fine. Renny gave him the family history, especially about her daughter Remy.

He slept well that night aided by a sleeping pill to defray travel fatigue and jet lag. While waiting the twenty minutes for it to work he lay thinking about what he was doing. He had had live-in servants for many years, what difference would it be to have one in a motor home with him?

Alfredo gave him a very warm welcome when he turned up at the yard in the morning. He came rushing out of the office closely followed by Remy and Renny. He opened the taxi boot and Remy immediately grabbed the suitcase and moved off towards the van standing nearby. By the time he had paid the taxi fare the luggage was lined up beside the campervan.

Alfredo unlocked the door and Remy waited for no one as she lugged the heavy case up the steps inside. She put it down and exclaimed, 'Oh, sir is this where we will live? It's beautiful.'

It truly was beautiful. A lush, thick dark cream carpet stretched the length of the van. The wooden paneling of doors and frames and cupboards was polished like a grand piano. Everything had the look of luxury about it.

'Not so fast, we have to talk.'

'I have to work, 'said Alfredo,' You can discuss everything together here,' and left them to it.

He had many questions and the first was, 'How did you get here?' It wasn't easy for a young woman to gain access to the USA. 'Do you mind if I see your passport?'

Everything was in order; she had a six-month visitor's visa. Alfredo had a Green Card, of which he was extremely proud and was able to sponsor the visit.

There were lots of questions about work experience and her plans for the future. Being a typical Filipino, she wanted to live in the USA and was hoping that her brother would be able to sponsor her one day. Meanwhile, she was planning to find a job in Manila and try to settle down after losing her husband. He was a soldier and had been killed in a skirmish with Muslim rebels in the south. There were no children. She had served in several homes of embassy people in Manila and knew about Western culture.

'What do you think you can do for me, if I decide to take you?' he asked.

'Oh, sir, I can cook, I love cooking, and I'll clean for you and do the laundry and ironing.'

'She's a beautician,' chimed in Renny, 'She'll cut your hair and do your nails and everything.' It looked as though he had passed the mother's test and scrutiny and was allowing a daughter to come.

Then there was the question of payment and he tried to explain that he was not expecting to employ a maid while he was on holiday but offered to pay her an allowance. He explained that he was not allowed to employ her so it had to be on the basis of pocket money only. What he was doing was simply giving her a working holiday. 'That's allright, sir,' said Alfredo, who had just returned to see how they were doing, 'provided it is enough.'

'Okay, what about five hundred dollars for a month. I'll pay all the expenses, food, travel, everything. And if I am very happy with you, I'll give you a generous tip at the end. But I do want to think about it a bit.'

Remy's face said it all, as a feeling of gratitude swept over her. She began to cry. 'Are you unhappy or happy, he asked.

'I'm so happy, sir, I am so happy. You will not be sorry about me sir. I will do everything, anything, sir,' the tears that had begun so quickly dried up just as fast.

So, it was settled. They would meet that night for dinner. It wasn't a bad idea to delay his departure for a day so he could be rested for the journey inland. Together with the two women he examined the camper van from one end to the other. It was the size of a small bus with permanent beds made up to sleep four with provision for two more-fold down bunks. There was a fully equipped kitchen, bathroom and toilet, TV and DVD player, air conditioner, and radio. Very comfortable, easy chairs and the driver's seat were an armchair.

It had a powerful diesel motor purportedly economical to run, a large water tank, gas for cooking, and a bank of batteries for power that when stationary was guaranteed to run all the electrics for three days without recharging. The fuel tank had a capacity of 100 liters that would take them nearly 1,000 kilometres. It had automatic stabilisers that levelled the van if parked on uneven ground. A GPS was fitted with the entire road network of North America.

He left the women chatting in the van while he went to the office to sign up. 'The GPS system will tell us where you are at all times. We put them in all our vehicles.' When he returned, he could tell by the looks on the women's faces that they had something to say but were embarrassed to ask.

Remy began, 'You are travelling alone, sir?' This she knew perfectly well, but was using the usual Philippine practice of stating the obvious. 'And there is lots of room here for many people.'

'Well, I wouldn't say much, but six at the most.'

'We are wondering that there is room for us both, sir, and we are thinking that perhaps we should both come with you.'

He should have seen this coming. They came from a country where many of their people live in very crowded conditions; privacy is not an important issue, the more the merrier. No one wants to be alone. In fact, it's the height of rudeness to leave a stranger or visitor alone. He recalled meeting a 42-year-old woman who told him that she had never been alone in her entire life. Always there was someone beside her day and night. To want to accompany him was simply being polite and shows a concern for him. It would also be a wonderful experience to travel in the USA in such a beautiful vehicle and he would pay for everything!

Another thing, they are both now single, are they both looking for a husband? Do they see me as a likely partner? Ah, but I'm not an American. These thoughts flashed through his mind in an instant as he sought for an answer to this question.

'Well, I will have to think about that. I wasn't even expecting one let alone two. Give me time to consider this.

My first thought is that it will cost me a lot more than I was expecting. Let me think about it for a while.' And think he did. Maybe mother doesn't want daughter to come with me, maybe mother wants to get her claws into me and is jealous of daughter. Does daughter really want mother to come? What am I getting myself into? Anyway, just now I need to unpack and settle in and he bent down to unlock the luggage. 'Let us do that for you sir.' He left them to it and returned to the office to buy a set of maps and travel guides and a directory of the all-important camping sites. He was told that all that information was on the GPS but he wanted a hard copy of it all. Within 10 minutes the women had unpacked his bag and placed the clothes in drawers and wardrobe. It was all done so quickly and neatly. I'm going across the road to that café for some coffee. Want to come with me?'

'No Sir, you go we will be here,' said Remy.

It was his first cup of what he called American coffee - black and quite weak, no guts to it, but much better for him than the strong stuff back home. What to do about these two? I can't take two. That's inviting trouble. There would be no peace. Two women talking away flat out in their usual way and probably in Tagalog. Even if they politely spoke quietly, it would not be the holiday he had envisioned - a time of quietness and reflection.

Seeing that he had already checked out of his hotel and had begun paying for the van, he decided to rest up in the van while still parked in the yard. He sent the women off inviting them to come back for dinner; they would meet up at the hotel.

He wondered at the wisdom of taking an unknown woman and living with her in a small place for a month! They both appeared to be of a quiet nature, very respectful, maybe even a bit fearful of him. But they seemed to understand the servant role so maybe it would be all right. He said to himself that he would soon know. He had hired many people over the years and felt that he could choose well. But which one? Certainly not both. I like them both. Then an idea came, what about changing over halfway! Mother first then daughter. Or should it be daughter first then mother.

He would see how Remy could handle a formal meal so invited the family for dinner at the hotel. But she was more at home than her brother. The array of cutlery did not confuse her as it did Alfredo, and even read the menu correctly advising her brother what to choose.

He had to decide by the end of the dinner. He studied both women as they ate together sizing them up, comparing one with the other. They were remarkably similar in height, body shape – both very sexy, unmarked faces and long luxuriant black hair. Their clothing was neat and although not expensive, they certainly were a cut above the average Filipina in her tee shirt and jeans. Both wore skirts and a blouse that did little to hide an ample bust. He decided that he liked them both and began to wonder if he should let them decide who should come. They were both very nice women. Maybe he would have more in common with the older one, yet perhaps the younger one would be more fun. But I'm not looking for fun he told himself. I just want a quiet interesting holiday. Dinner was soon over so he decided that it would be easier for everyone if Alfredo called him in the morning to hear his decision.

After wishing them good night he watched them walk away chatting together. He took a sleeping pill and was soon asleep.

He awoke to the strident ring of the phone. It was 9 am and Alfredo's cheery voice greeted him. 'What do you think, sir?'

'Well, Alfredo, what do you think? Both your mother and sister are lovely women, I like them both but only one can come with me.'

'Well, sir in that case you had better take my sister. My mother likes you and feels happy about Remy going with you. She was worried about it, but not anymore.'

'Okay, maybe you are right, send her to me this morning and we will leave right away.'

'Yes, sir, I will, but she is already here. We thought that was what you would do.'

He dressed and opened the door of the van, and there was Remy standing nearby, smiling from ear to ear. He called her over and invited her to unpack and settle in. 'Oh, thank you, sir, I am sure you will be very happy with me, I will help you a lot and do anything for you. Do you want some coffee, have you eaten breakfast yet?

'No, not yet, there is no food here. We will leave straight away and find some food. Say goodbye to your brother and we will be off,' as he started the motor. Immediately Alfredo appeared at his window to send them off. Remy was busy looking in all the cupboards so he had to tell her that while they were moving, she must be seated.

CHAPTER TWO

They headed out of the city on the road that led to Pasadena. 'Keep a look out for a supermarket and a place where we can eat breakfast,' he called. Remy came forward and sat in the front seat. They soon came across a huge shopping center complete with a supermarket that eclipsed anything either of them had ever seen.

They went straight to a coffee shop and ordered a breakfast. 'We need to make a list of what we need,' he said, taking a small notebook from his pocket. 'There's nothing in the van so we need everything.'

'Chicken, oil, salt, pepper, seasoning, bread, butter,' began Remy.

'Oh, forget it,' he said, let's walk around here and we'll see everything we need. One large supermarket trolley filled to brim later, they checked out at number 36 of the 50 cash registers.

Let's put everything in the van quickly and sort it out later,' he said. They hadn't quite finished unloading when a man sauntered up and said, 'Where she going. You got a lot of stuff there; you are going to need help to eat it all. He grabbed a bag and made to enter the van when he was stopped. Joe snatched the bag from him and said, 'Thank you very much but we are quite ok thanks.'

'Oh, you sure you are all right. Where you go? Mind if I come for a ride? You off to the desert? I like the desert. It's a mighty dangerous place the desert and you'll need my help.'

'Thank you very much, but we are quite ok. Please leave us thank you.'

At that moment a police car pulled up beside them. An officer leaned out of the window and said, 'You folks all right?'

'Yes, we're ok officer, just telling this man we don't need his help.' The policeman looked at the man carefully and clearly didn't like what he saw. Then said, 'You get any trouble just call us.'

'Thanks, we will.'

'Dirty pigs always sniffing around making' trouble,' and then unlocked the car right next to them and got in. But he didn't move off, just sat there and watched. Joe didn't like it all. He ordered Remy to take a seat and moved out of the parking lot. Five minutes later he noticed that same car following them a half a mile back. He was on the main road out of town now coming close to Pasadena.

'Don't look around, but look in the mirrors, is that man in the blue car still following us?

She leaned forward and peered into the wing mirror, 'Yes sir, he's there.'

'I am going to stop and call the police.'

After checking the police emergency number, he tried to make the operator understand his predicament. Speaking slowly, he said for the third time,' I am parked outside 34756 Highway Boulevard, Pasadena. I am in a large trailer number Ca238876. A man in a blue car is following me and threatening me. Can you please send someone to chase him away?'

'What is he doing? How is he threatening you? Oh, he's just driving behind you, that's all right sir, he can do that, just call us if he does anything bad.'

He drove on for another thirty minutes and the blue car kept well back. What to do? Joe drove into a suburban residential area of Pasadena up and down streets of beautiful homes and then back out onto the highway. Still the blue car followed.

'Look out for a police station,' called Joe.

'There's a police car,' cried Remy. 'Stop him.'

Joe flashed the headlights, blew the horn and waved out to the car as it approached and pulled to the side. Joe opened the door and began to get out. A policeman called out, 'Stay there. What's wrong?'

Joe began to shout across the traffic, then waved the cop over to him. He slowly got out if the car and sauntered across the road. 'What's the trouble man?'

'You see that blue car back there. He has been following me ever since I stopped at a supermarket back there. He wanted to come with us and I refused so he's just been following me for half an hour. I don't like it'.

The policeman looked down the road, then drawled, 'Well, I don't see any blue car back there. You sure of this?'

'Yes of course, I'm sure. I have already called 911 and they said he can follow us if he wants to but call them if he did anything bad.'

'Well, he's gone now. We'll take a look. You go, you'll be all right.'

What a start for a holiday. He looked across at Remy. 'I'm sorry about this, I hope you are not frightened.'

'Oh no sir, American police are very good, I have seen them many times on TV.'

Joe drove on for a few minutes, then down a side street and took out his maps. Maybe it would be better not to head for the desert just yet. He decided to go further up the coast road and forget the desert for a few days.

He handed the campsites book to her and said, testing

her, 'Find me a campsite in the next town from here, which is north of Pasadena,' and continued to study his map. It only took her about three minutes. 'Looks like I won't need to use this GPS while you are around.'

The campsite was equipped with all modern conveniences but being fully independent Joe only needed a suitable parking space. The curator was a little perturbed at the way Joe insisted they park out of sight of the road and not use what he called a luxury park close to the amenities.

'OK, it's nearly lunchtime. What can you cook for lunch? I am going for a walk while you prepare the meal.'

After making sure Remy could handle the stove and all the equipment he left her to it, giving her an hour to prepare a meal. He was a bit worried about her using gas, but she seemed to have had enough experience with it. Remy responded with 'Oh, Sir I can cook for you. What would you like?'

'What about a hamburger with salad,' not wanting to make the test too difficult, 'and keep the windows open while you are cooking.'

On his way back from his walk the curator came over and wanted to talk. He said he knew this van. It had been custom built for a family who had used it only once before they split up. 'It was terrible, mum went one way and dad the other and left the children in the middle. They had to go into foster care. They came from this place, lived just over there. I rented this out through the hire company on his behalf. You know, this van has only been used a couple of times, it's last year's model and they could never agree where to go with it. You never saw such a disagreeable couple.'

He went over to the van and knelt down near the rear axle. 'Did they tell you what was in here? Come here and look carefully.' Near the wheel cavity was a small door. 'Open that and see what you can find. Use the key with the ignition lock.' Sure enough, Joe opened the lock and the door fell open. Inside he could see something wrapped in white linen.

'Looks like a gun.'

'It sure is buddy. That bloke was a hunter.'

'I don't need this; I'd better take it back. I'd need a licence, wouldn't I? What if the police found this on me?'

'Aw, go on, they'll never find it hidden in there. Just leave it. Anyway, this is a rental, it's not your responsibility. If you don't touch it no one will know.'

It truly was a fine gun. Lightly oiled and enclosed in fine linen and even Joe, who didn't know much about guns could see it was a special piece. The curator carefully checked it and announced that it had nine bullets, including one ready to fire. 'Look, see this is the safety catch, make sure it is always on and you'll have no worries. And if a grizzly bear comes after you or a bad man, you'll be ready for him,' he grinned and wrapped it up and carefully inserted it into the cavity and locked the door.

As Joe entered the van Remy called to say that the meal was ready. There on the table, neatly set out was a luscious looking hamburger that was trying to look like a homemade Big Mac. But there was only one table setting and one hamburger. 'Hey, is that for us both? Surely not, where's yours?'

'Oh, sir, you eat first, I will have mine later.' He knew exactly what was happening. Remy had been taught that the master ate first and alone and the servant later, never together.

Joe sat down and called her to him. 'Please sit and listen to me. I know you offered to be my maid and I know that maids eat later. But not this time. I want you to have a holiday with me, we will always eat together and do things together. We will eat together in a restaurant or go to the movies together. It's not me and you, it's us. I am not paying you like a maid, it's just pocket money, we will be like family, like you are my daughter. Now go and make your lunch. I'll go ahead and eat mine while it is hot, but next time it is us together. Understand?'

'You are so kind sir. Thank you, sir.'

'Now that's another thing. I think it is better if you called me Joe, not sir all the time. I know you are being respectful but I'd like it if you call me Joe.'

'Yes, sir..er...yes, Joe.'

After they had eaten Joe said that he needed to rest, and Remy too seemed a little tired still suffering from jet plane fatigue. Joe said, 'That's my bed there, the big one under the front window. You can sleep where you like. There are four beds to choose from.' Remy modestly chose one at the other end of the van. It had a curtain shielding it. That was perfect for her.

They both slept for four hours. When Remy offered to cook chicken drumsticks for dinner it reminded Joe of the way some Filipinas cook them in a frying pan with the fat spurting out all over the place. So, he patiently explained how he wanted her to use a lid on the frying pan otherwise the van would soon reek of fat.

He showed her all the facilities of the van and emphasized the need to conserve water and power. It truly was a luxury vehicle. Every fitting was of the highest quality. There was an all-around sound connected to the DVD and TV. An automatic antenna system found local and satellite TV and radio broadcasters quickly and accurately. The driving cab was like an airplane cockpit, a mass of buttons and controls. There was an inbuilt no-hands cell phone with controls on the steering wheel and a hand piece beside each bed, table and lounge. There were three video cameras. One in the front so positioned to give a view of parking and a second one at the rear. A third gave a view of the road behind. The GPS was accurate to one meter.

There was a library of 50 of the latest movies on DVD and another 50 of music of all kinds. A good quality notebook computer with wireless broadband was hidden away in a pullout drawer. The vehicle was fully air-conditioned and had under floor heating. The bedding was of the finest quality, and there was a shelf of paperbacks of every description. The emergency medical kit appeared to cater for any need usually handled without a doctor. The bathroom was equipped like the one at home with a large range of toiletries.

In another drawer he found some powerful Leica binoculars and in the back of the wardrobe a 2-inch telescope. Hidden away in a soundproof compartment under the rear was an onboard generator.

'I won't want to give this up,' mumbled Joe under his breath. Remy heard him and said, 'When my mom hears about this, she is going to be so jealous of me.'

While Remy cooked the meal, Joe busied himself with the large file of instructions regarding all the on-board equipment. There was even an extensive survival manual should they break down in the desert or in a forest. Under the van was a container with emergency firewood, matches, a spade and an ax and what looked like a few packages of army emergency 'C' rations. There was a whole chapter about the danger of bears. Placed next to this was a toolbox and two spare tires, and in another box, a set of snow chains and a large lantern with a flashing red light.

After the meal Joe lay on the bed and stretched and yawned. 'This is jet lag and travel fatigue setting in, I'm tired, but not sleepy.'

'Joe, I can help you, let me give you a soothing massage, it will help you relax and sleep.

She applied lotion to the arms and began to rub and scrub pulling at the hairs. His skin had become quite dry.

Overall, it was a pleasant sensation to have one's body covered in oil then massaged. Rubbing the hairs on his slightly hairy legs didn't hurt it was just the arms. He was lying in his shorts on the bed covered across the middle with a sarong that Remy produced from her voluminous bag. It was made of the smoothest, softest material he had ever seen. But she was careful and skillful this woman.

He lay on his stomach and she began to oil the feet and legs. Her strong hands pressed deeply into the flesh and she would trace each muscle with long strokes. After massaging the buttocks, she covered them with the sarong. He was thinking 'what sort of a girl is this?' But she was very proper in her work, no funny business. On the whole the massage was harder than he expected after all it was the dry skin that was the problem not deep muscle tissue. She pulled up the sheet and blankets and quietly said, 'You sleep now. Goodnight,' and bent and lightly kissed him on the forehead. What have I let myself in for he wondered and immediately fell into a deep sleep?

Next day as they were passing the 10,000 f.a.s.l. Mount Baldy in the San Bernardino Mountains, it had no trees on the summit. He asked Remy, 'Do you know about the speed of light?' She looked puzzled. Obviously, a new concept to her. Then after a moment's thought said, 'Yes, I have heard of it, but I don't know anything about it.'

'Well about 80 years ago a scientist based 22 miles away over there focussed a beam of light onto this mountain and measured how fast light can travel. If you look up the Lonely Planet Guide on the shelf, there you will see how fast it goes.' She opened the book at the place where he had marked it and found that light travelled at 299,796 kilometers per second. 'You know; it takes 8 minutes to travel from the earth to the sun at the speed of light?'

Joe's real interest was the railroad and he soon found a spot beside a railroad line to watch the steady procession of long freights. After a few minutes he took out a camera and walked a short distance to a small rise beside the track and waited for the next train. Being a retired professional photographer, his cameras were a little larger than usual, and thus quite obvious.

He was lining up a shot of the next train when a sharp siren sounded right behind him. A police car had come up quietly and sounded the siren to attract his attention. It nearly frightened him to death.

'And what do you think you are doing,' said an officer who looked like he had come from over the southern border, 'Don't you know it's illegal to photograph trains?'

'Sorry, but the man who rented me this van said that it was quite ok to photograph anything in the USA provided it was not done in a suspicious manner. What's suspicious about me? I have passed several people photographing trains along this road. Anyway, I'm from New Zealand and I love railroads and you have some wonderful ones here.'

'Driver's licence please and the papers for this vehicle and your passport.' Remy looked out the van door, and the cop said, 'Who's that you got there?'

Then began a long check of passports, visas, vehicle papers and driver's licence. Fortunately, Remy's were in order otherwise they could have been in real trouble. But he thought he had found something wrong when he noted that Joe's licence did not include heavy traffic vehicles. He began to make a fuss when Joe pointed out that the vehicle was 6 inches short of a heavy vehicle description therefore his licence was valid. He had to admit, it was a large three-axle vehicle like a bus. Everything else was ok, but the cop was very suspicious of Remy.

Joe did not know very much about Mexican temperament, but he was worried that he had won one round and might get a nasty response. The cop had lost face badly. I must let him win something, he thought.

Then Joe said, 'If you don't like my photographing here, then I can delete the photos easily right now. I've only just arrived in the country and have only taken two shots.'

The officer gazed at him steadily for a minute. 'Please tell me what I can and cannot photograph here. I'm only interested in the railroad. Let me get you something from the van that might help.' He had a copy of a special magazine called *Vacation Train Spotting in the USA*.

'No, you stay right here, I haven't finished with you yet,' snarled the cop. But for another minute or two he said nothing but just stared at them both. Joe stared back at him. He looked down at the policeman's boots and stared at them. This was an old trick he had learned in Africa. There is something very disconcerting by staring at a person's feet. He looked at one foot and then the other. Finally, the cop said, 'you had better come with me to the station.'

'But why do we have to do that? I am sure your boss will be very interested in a magazine published here in California that explains to tourists where are the best places to see the trains, and photograph them.' He looked at the officer very carefully and said not unkindly, 'I think you had better see it first because it might save you a wee bit of trouble if you are considered to be worrying tourists unnecessarily.'

'Bring it,' he snapped.

'See who published this, your own California Tourist Board. Are you thinking they don't know the law? And look at the date, January this year, well over 9/11.

'Look, sir, you are doing your job, I know that, but I can assure you that we are no danger to your state and country.'

'What about this woman? She has no work permit.'

'No, that's true, but she's on holiday and not working. She has become my girlfriend and is having a holiday with me.'

The officer suddenly turned on his heel and without a word marched back to his car and drove off.

'Let's get out of this fellow's district,' and they headed down the road on to Victorville and then west towards Apple Valley.'

'So, I'm your girlfriend, am I. That's nice.'

'I think you know what I mean, that was just to get us out of trouble.'

'Yes, I know...but it was nice.'

The first thing they noticed was this was not a city, but called itself a town. No one was likely to forget when visiting this place that it was the home of Roy and Dale Rogers. Their names are everywhere. They helped to set up a church, a detention home for boys and are said to have raised between 20 and 40 children as their own. Apple Valley is on the southern edge of the Mojave Desert and apparently a lady planted three apple trees in her yard to prove that it was a good place for fruit trees and called it Apple Valley.

He found a quiet spot where they could park up for a while. 'Now Remy, I want you to tell me about your family. It is nice that your mother could come with you to the USA and I'm sorry she couldn't come with us.'

'Well Joe,' said Remy, as she curled her legs up under her, 'my father died about ten years ago. He was a soldier and was killed by Moro Muslim rebels in the South. But he was a hard man and drank too much. Maybe it was his work because they gave him some tough jobs to do. Like when they wanted to build a railway in Manila, he was in charge of a group that had to chase people out of their houses so they could destroy them and build the railway. Of course, the people objected and there were many fights and he had to shoot at some of them. He wasn't supposed to tell anyone about that or Marcos would have shot him. He used to come home very angry and upset and drink so much he would fall down.

'In one of those shanty houses he found a woman who was about to give birth. He was supposed to chase her out, but he couldn't. He called his commander but was told to get on with it. He told one of his men to call the army ambulance and while he was arguing with the controller, my father snatched the phone and demanded an ambulance immediately. "We are military," he was told. So dad said, "it's one of my people and has very serious stomach pains I need him attended to right away." When the ambulance came without waiting for the driver to even open the door dad pushed the woman inside and onto to the bed. She was screaming because her baby was coming. She had it in the ambulance. He got into trouble with his officer for that, but he was a family man and after the official reprimand by his commanding officer, he gave dad a very unmilitary wink as he left his office and told him not to do anything like that again.'

'Was he a good father to you?'

'Yes of course he was. In fact, when my uncle tried to abuse me, my father shot him in the leg.'

'Wow, that's sounds like a real story, tell me about it. Do you mind or does that upset you?'

'My uncle came to stay with us sometimes and he had no job. He was always in the house. One day when I came home from school, I found him lying on my bed. He was drunk. So, I hit him with my school bag and told him to get out. He jumped up and grabbed me and threw me onto the bed. He was shouting at me saying that I was a little tramp and that he would teach me something I would never forget. He pulled on my clothes and tore my best dress for school. It was a very nice one that my mother sewed for me and I was very proud of it. It tore all the way down the front and he could see my underclothes. He grabbed my bra and started pulling. It hurt a lot and he couldn't pull it off because, you know, bras are very strong and you can't just tear them. He was pulling at them and I got off the bed and was bouncing around the room yelling my head off. His dirty fingernails were sharp and they were hurting my breast.

'Just then my father came home and when he saw us, he yelled at my uncle to stop but he wouldn't. Dad could see what was happening so he pulled out his 45 SAP and said, "Stop or I'll shoot."

'"Naw, you won't shoot your daughter."

'But my dad fired and hit him in the leg. He let go of me and screamed, "You've shot me, you've shot me," and he held onto his leg trying to stop the blood. It oozed out between his fingers and down his leg.

'Dad told me to get some cloth and he tied it on like a bandage. When he had finished, he said to my uncle, "You get out of this house and do not come back again. If you tell anyone who shot you, I will come and find you and do it again. Now go. I've still got 6 bullets left."

'Well of course the pain in his leg was so great he couldn't go anywhere. Just then Mother came home. She already knew what had happened because the maid had met her at the gate and told her that her brother had been shot by dad.

'Of course, she had pity on her brother so she told dad that they had better let him stay for a bit while the leg healed. She undid the bandage and checked to see if the bullet had come out. She said they had to clean the wound and the only thing we had in the house was dad's whisky. She poured it over the wound and uncle yelled out because it stung him. Then she bandaged him up again and told him to lie quietly for a while. She put a mat in the passage and told him to lie there.

'Mum and dad then began to argue as to what to do about him. If he went to a doctor, he would have to report a gunshot wound to the police. Dad said it was a clean wound as the bullet had gone straight through and should heal ok so there was no need for a doctor. He had seen plenty of wounds like that. If the police heard about it, then they might charge uncle for assault or even rape and that would bring great shame on the family, let alone me.

'Fortunately, the maid was out of the house and came back just as the shot went off so she didn't see exactly what had happened. Mum talked to her very strongly and told her that there had been an accident with dad's gun and that she mustn't talk about it to anyone. At that time, we were living in a private street not in the military compound so that made it easier for us. She was a good woman and had been with our family since I was a baby.

'I was feeling very scared and shaking all the time, so my maid came to me and put her arms around me and comforted me. She could see that my dress was torn badly and asked me how that happened. I told her we were fighting at school and that's where it happened. My dress came open a little and she saw the scratch marks down my front. She looked at me and then said, "I see." But what she could see was something else. She could see the truth of it all. Then she whispered in my ear, "I will ask Mum to send her brother away. He's not a good man. I think he deserved the bullet."

'Many weeks later when calm had been restored to the family, my maid told me that uncle had tried to rape her one night when we were all away. The second night he was with us he went to her room and knocked on the door. 'I stupidly unlocked it and opened it and there he was. He stepped past me into the room and said, "Don't worry, I only want to talk. Leave the door open and switch on the light. You will be ok."

'He sat down on my bed because my chair had been damaged and was not in the room. I sat down too, as far away as possible. He said that he just wanted to talk. He just talked about the family and his old job, nothing much really and after half an hour got up and left the room.'

'Next night the same thing happened. Exactly the same. The third night he came dressed only his boxer shorts. I told him I was too tired to talk and asked him to leave. He pushed his way into the room told me to lie down on the bed. He then sat down and tried to put his arm around me. "I want to kiss you,' "he said. "Just a little kiss on your head, and eyes, and cheeks, and neck and...."

'Get out I yelled and turned my back to him. He suddenly put his hand under my tee shirt and grabbed my breast and began to squeeze it gently. I made my hand into a fist and suddenly turned and punched him as hard as I could. I hit him in the stomach and he went whoosh and fell onto the floor all doubled up.'

'She must have hit him in the solar plexus that would slow him up.'

'Yes, it was, and after a few minutes he got up and went outside. Next day he said to the maid, 'I can still feel you in my hand.'

'Get away from me,' she screamed at him. My mother heard her and wanted to know what the matter was, but she just said that she had to get on with her work and could not talk about him.'

'Your father was killed by the Moro rebels; how did that happen?'

Joe was amazed at her knowledge of this many years

old conflict. She explained that they were called the Moro Islamic Liberation Front and that they want separation from the rest of the Philippines. The problem is that there are four and a half million Muslims in the country so it's a big group. They have been fighting for about 40 years. Several peace accords have been broken and many lives lost something like 120,000. She explained that she knew a lot about this because at the time her father was transferred south one of her teachers came from Zamboanga and he spent a lot of time helping Remy and her family to understand what was happening there.

The local people were called Chavancano and they were fiercely proud of the fact that they were the first people to live in the area. The Spanish came in 1635 and they were followed by Malays, Chinese and Arabs. That's when Islam came. Remy's father tried to befriend some of the local people and learn their language that was a Spanish Creole because he thought that if he was supposed to help protect them, he had better understand them better. He had been there only three months when his platoon was caught in a Moro ambush in a thick forest. The men not killed in the fire fight were later beheaded and Remy said that she has always hoped that her father was killed instantly by a bullet and not beheaded. 'Sure, he was a tough man but he was my father and I'll never forget what he did to save me.'

'I know a little about that place because I was there a few years ago. I came by van over from Cipato and I had to lie on the floor all the way because at that time the Moros were kidnapping foreigners. My colleagues would not let me out of their sight and when I went out on the street in Zamboanga there was always someone with me walking like bodyguards, one in the front and one at my back and a third guy carried my cameras.

'My back was sore after the unpleasant ride on the van floor so I sneaked out of the hotel when my guard wasn't looking and went into the massage parlor that I had noticed earlier that was right next door to the hotel. The woman there gave me a really good going over and soothed away my aches.'

Joe got up to stretch his legs and walked the length of the van then returned to find Remy silently weeping. Her body shook and the tears streamed down her face, but she was quite silent. He went to her and pulled her to her feet and, smothering her with his arms said quietly, 'I am sorry to upset you by letting you talk about sad times.' He gave her his clean white handkerchief,' quietly thankful he had a decent one in his pocket.

After a few minutes she sobbed, 'I'm sorry Sir, I mean Joe, but sometimes I feel sad about my dad. But there is something else I must tell you. You see, a few weeks after my uncle's attack on me they transferred my father to the south. We are sure that this was the army's way of covering up the shooting. We think that, somehow, dad's commander heard about it and quietly moved him away. So, you see it's all my fault that he died.'

It took Joe several minutes to quieten and comfort her and assure her that from what he could understand it surely wasn't her fault at all.

'It's nearly dinner time what shall we eat?' Remy wiped her eyes and blew her nose and said, 'Let me do it. Let me surprise you.'

'Please do and I'll check my email.'

After they had eaten Remy began to wash the dishes. Joe took a tea towel and began to dry them. She stopped and turned to him saying, 'Joe this is my job, you don't have to do this. Please sit down.' Normally he would have insisted on helping but the pleading look she gave him signalled that he ought to leave them to her. He did so thinking that he was now back in the good old days when the servants did everything and to try and help was usually an insult to them.

When she was finished, he said, 'you haven't told me anything about yourself yet. What about your education, your work experience, your boyfriends, your husband?'

'If I tell you about myself, will you tell me about yourself?'

'Of course. Let's start with education.' The details of her schooling tripped of her tongue. Manila based kindergarten, grade school, high school, university gradings poured out with details of each subject. The university degree interested him. It seemed to be mainly in the field of home economics, which explained why she had made such good progress as a housekeeper. After graduation, she obtained a position in the home of an American junior diplomat and a few years later became the senior housekeeper for the American Ambassador.

In the meantime, her mother had become the housekeeper at the presidential palace when Mrs. Aquino was head of state. Ah, thought Joe, that's how this family is all here in the USA now. They knew how to pull the strings.

'I've been to the palace,' said Joe, 'and met Mrs. Aquino. She was a very nice lady. You know, we were standing in the lounge of the palace and suddenly we heard a voice behind us saying, 'hullo' and there was the president walking down the stairs. I was there to photograph a committee that was being sworn in and she was so friendly to everyone.'

'She was so sweet to my mother and all the staff and I was hoping to get a job there, but after she went, we didn't know anyone so it was hopeless.'

'Yeah, that's right; it has always been 'it's not what you know, but who you know.' Where's your mother now?'

'She's housekeeper at the British Embassy.'

'I bet that's a lot different to the Americans.'

'Oh yes, they are completely different. Their food, their customs, everything. But they are very nice though, and treat my mother well. In fact, the ambassador's wife was very fond of her computer and she taught my mother how to use one. She was a schoolteacher and loved to teach people so when she discovered that my mum did not have a computer, she jumped at the chance to teach her. She was a lovely lady and often would go to the local school and help the teachers. She was always in the kitchen teaching the cook how to cook!'

'How come you are in the States for six months?'
'I was lucky enough to get 6 months leave of absence. But I haven't told you about my brother, not Alfredo, you know him. But my older brother was killed in the military. It was those horrible Muslim things in the south. He got caught in an explosion at a camp. They blew up the ammunition. He was on guard there and they came in the night and killed all the guards then blew it up.'

'When did that happen?'

'It's six years now, but we still miss him. He was just about to get married. His fiancé was a lovely girl who had no family so my mother asked her to come and live with us and become a daughter anyway. I call her my sister, my real sister not a sister-in-law.'

'She's been with you for six years. Doesn't she want to marry someone else?'

'No, no, she won't even talk to any boys, she's still in love with my brother. However, I do have a cousin who is very interested in her and he is slowly winning her love. Mother and I are advising her to marry him, and I think she will sometime soon. He has been a security guard for a while and now he has become the manager of the company so he's got a good job.'

Without another word Remy got up and went to her bed, pulling the curtain and then slumped down. Soon

Joe could hear a quiet sobbing. He let her cry for a few minutes, then went to her. 'Remy,' he whispered, 'Let me come in.' Without waiting for an answer, he pulled aside the curtain and stood over her. 'Remy, I know you are very sad, but you must try and move ahead with your life.' He bent down and cradled her head in his arms trying to comfort her as well as he could. He dried her eyes with his handkerchief. He began to gently massage her neck and shoulders. Gradually the sobs subsided she turned her face to him and kissed him on the cheek, 'Thank you, you are so kind.'

'You sleep now and I will move the van to a safe place for the night.' He bent and kissed her on the forehead. 'Goodnight,' he whispered.

Joe took the opportunity to read through some of the literature given to him by the agency. He discovered that it is against the law in the USA to drive off in a motor home the same day that you arrive in the country. There were pages and pages of advice to people trying to settle into a RV vehicle for a holiday. Like 'learning to live with 30 amps.' And 'what to pack' – it was a bit late for that.

He woke the next morning to the smell of coffee and toast cooking. He piped up over his covers and silently watched Remy setting the table. She was dressed only in her thin nighty and he could see the outline of her body against the window light. There was no doubt she was a beautiful woman. 'Is that coffee I can smell?' She looked up alarmed and scurried back to her corner to dress.

'You woke up too early. I will shower and please you eat your breakfast.'

CHAPTER THREE

On the road again, they headed for Tehachapi Pass. This was something Joe wanted to see as the railroad line threads its way over the hills. According to his railroad guide there were special railroad viewing sites where he could photograph and watch the trains without hassles from the police. In fact, it is considered one of the prime rail fan areas of the country.

They soon found a commodious spot that was already occupied by half a dozen vehicles of various types. The men were all leaning over the viewing railings and the women were mostly in the vehicles waiting for their men to have their fill of huge diesel locomotives hauling countless freight wagons over the hill and around and through the spiral where the train passes over itself.

'This is very interesting,' said Joe. 'All the men are watching the trains and the women are inside reading books or listening to music.'

Carefully, Joe explained to Remy that he was a former railroad man and he was in the USA primarily to view trains and that they would spend the rest of the day here. He thought it best to lay down the law right at the beginning and say, 'I want no complaints from you about stopping to watch trains.' At the same time thinking, she is not my maid yet she is my maid so she has no say in what I do, but I guess I have to be reasonable.

Remy looked offended. 'Joe, of course you do what you want don't ask me, I'm just here to help you.' He squeezed her hand and said, 'Thanks. But maybe there will be things you would like to do and see. Just tell me if there is. I want you to enjoy this trip.'

He was soon in conversation with other men avidly watching the sight of 85 wagons being hauled up the pass through the 8,000-foot mountains. He was soon told that this was the busiest single-track railway in the USA.

Joe had always wanted to go camping in the desert so they set out on the road through the desert looking for a suitable camping spot. It was illegal to take the heavy van off a tar sealed road so he had to be content with a relatively open area and not go too far off the road. After an hour he came across a flat dry area between two hills. It was possible to park the van in a safe place, but out of sight of the main road as it was on a curve. It was a perfect place. The desert was out to the side and the slightly elevated parking space gave a great view of the wide-open spaces. There were no mountains in sight beyond the road. Maybe there would be sightings of wildlife. The sun would set behind them, but he could expect a beautiful sight when the sun came up across the desert plain.

While Remy prepared a meal, Joe studied the guidebooks. There were about 89 species of animals and a host of insects. Most of the animals were nocturnal so he'd have to sit up all night if he hoped to see any of them. The full moon was near so he might be in luck. There were 30 types of birds.

After dinner they sat outside on camp chairs and enjoyed the tranquillity of the place. There were only a couple of vehicles every hour the sounds of which quickly dissipated in the still evening air.

Joe awoke to a strange sound beneath the floor. Was it an animal, surely not a person? He lay still listening. It moved slowly and gradually quietened. He took his high-powered 'flashlight' as Alfredo described it, but really was a lantern with a kilometre-long beam. He quietly went to the door and opened it cautiously, swinging the lamp around in a semicircle, and the under the van. Nothing. He walked around to the other side, but saw nothing untoward.

It must have been an animal, maybe a stray dog or even an exotic a coyote. He refocused on the view ahead out across the desert. Slowly he brought the beam around wondering if he might spot a wild animal. Here and there a pair of eyes glistened in the light but he had no idea what they were. Perhaps a feral cat, a rabbit could be any of the many species out there. They were all too far away to distinguish a body, only the eyes. In one area there were several glistening in the light and doubtless this was a pack of coyotes.

'Did you hear any strange noises last night?' he asked Remy at breakfast. She'd heard nothing but had slept soundly. 'Apart from me snoring of course.'

'Oh Joe, of course you can snore. You are a man. My mother said that you must always let a man snore because at least you have got one of your own.' That was the most comforting thing he had ever heard about this quite vexing subject and thought again of his dear wife who put up with him for so long.

There was another small road that led further into the desert and they soon found another suitable spot to camp. It was several miles from the main road and being a single track, albeit a tarred road, it appeared to be rarely used.

They spent the afternoon dozing and reading with Remy about every hour asking if Joe required a drink or something.

He had been lying on the bed for a sleep when he was awakened by Remy gently massaging his brow. 'Your skin is still dry it needs more treatment. Let me do it.'

'OK, go ahead but don't wake me up.'

'Silly, you are awake, but go to sleep again. I will give you my sleepy one.'

She pulled the cover off him and pushed him over onto his stomach. His tee shirt and pants came off easily and she began to massage his neck and shoulders. It was a different cream this time with a gentle lavender scent. 'Just relax,' she whispered, 'Go to sleep.' It was amazing the effect of this cream. He began to doze. He was conscious of her hands carefully and gently smoothing away his cares, but importantly, cleansing and revitalizing his skin. The last thing he knew was her hands on his buttocks and then sliding down his legs to his feet and toes.

An hour later he woke up to find himself lying naked on the bed covered by her sarong. He had been sleeping on his stomach, something that he never did.

He raised his head to see Remy sitting at the table watching him. 'My, you have wonderful hands. Massages usually wake me up but yours put me to sleep.'

'It's all about the cream we use. You want to sleep I can make you sleep. You want to wake up, I can do that too. You want sex, I can make you want even an old lady. You want no sex; I can do that too.'

'Where did you learn all that stuff? Who taught you? I thought you were just a hairdresser and a beautician as well as a house maid, err a house manager or whatever you did.'

She held up her book ready to throw it at him. 'I'm much more than you think I am.'

'Come on, tell me more about it. Who was your teacher?'

'I have an aunty who is a healer. Not one of those miraculous ones like you see on TV but she was trained in native medicine. Her knowledge of plants and herbs and trees is amazing. She spends a lot of time walking in the forest near where she lives and makes up her own potions and medicines. Her daughter, my cousin, is also very good and aunty says will become a famous healer one day.'

Remy went to a cupboard and produced a small leather

bag and showed Joe her collection. 'What are they all for?'

'This one is for sleep, this one no sleep like wake up, this one for sex, this one no sex, this one for skin massage, and this for muscle massage.'

'What's that one?'

'No, no, not for you, only for women.' Better not ask any more thought Joe.

'Maybe we had better use this one while you are with me,' said Joe pointing to the no sex one.

'You are very naughty,' she replied blushing deeply.

'You Filipino people look so pretty when you blush, makes your *kayumangi* skin looks so nice.'

She thumped him on the arm and put the bag away and turned back to him. 'How did you know kayumangi? That's Tagalog for our skin colour.

'You may be surprised but I know all sorts of things, like *Mahal na mahal kita.*'

'You know that? How many women have you said that to?'

'Oh, I can say I love you in a lot of languages. If you were an Indonesian, I would say *saya cinta padamu.* I had a Bicol girlfriend once and I could say to her *namumutan ta ka.* And to my Thai friend I would say *phom rak khun.* '

'Do you want to hear some more I love you?

'I think you have had so many girlfriends all over the world, you must have, and you are such a kind man.'

'Well, thanks, but all you have to do is go to the web and Google 'I love you in many languages.' I found one that was a bit like something from the South Pacific. In Albanian, you know Albania, its in Europe. One word, *duo*, sounds like number two doesn't it? Imagine telling your girlfriend or your wife 'Darling you are *te dua* my number two!'

'I think we had better change the subject,' said Remy. 'What do you want for dinner?'

'What am I paying you for, you are supposed to decide that' replied Joe grabbing the binoculars as he stepped out the door. 'I'm going for a walk, be back soon.'

He climbed the hill to the right side of the van from where he had a good view of the plain. It was possible to see the place where the road he was on left the main road. There was a car in the distance and he watched it carefully. It turned onto his road and it soon appeared to be an old blue Japanese car of some sort. As it came closer, he felt a surge of alarm, surely not, yes it was, it was the blue car that was parked next to them at the supermarket. He slowly moved carefully to screen himself behind some bushes.

With luck, he wouldn't see their caravan and he waited, holding his breath as the car made its way very slowly down the road. He stayed hidden as he watched it drive past their park. The road went straight across the plain for about a mile then turned left into a hilly section. Joe waited another hour until he was sure that it would not return.

But it was a worry. How could this fellow know where they were? How come he chose the right part of this seemingly endless desert? He couldn't see the driver properly but he was sure it was the same one who wanted to come with them. The car had the same broken roof rack, yes it surely was the same one.

'Joe, dinner is ready,' called Remy. As they ate Remy said, 'What's the matter Joe? Is there something wrong? Have I upset you?

'No, no, nothing. It's nothing.'

'It's not nothing, it's something. What is it? Since you came back you have been quiet and look so worried.'

After watching a DVD, they went to bed. But Joe couldn't sleep. Where was that fellow? Will he come back? After an hour he quietly took the lantern and cell phone and looked outside. There was enough moonlight to see so he climbed the hill again without using the light. It was then that he remembered he hadn't locked the door. But there was a signal for the phone.

He watched and waited for an hour and, feeling the desert cold get to him, slowly returned to the van. As he approached the door, he could hear a muffled sound, like someone trying to cry out through a gag. He listened carefully. That wasn't a DVD or the TV, that was Remy. He looked around for something to use as a weapon and then realised that the lantern had a few sharp edges, it would do nicely as a club.

His hand was on the door when he remembered the gun stowed underneath in its secret compartment. He quickly retrieved it. Slowly he turned the door handle. But it was locked from the inside.

'Remy are you all right? Open the door.'

Silence inside. Then a muffled squeal. 'Shuddup you bitch.' Yes, that was his voice. The sound came from the end of the van. There's only one thing to do, and that's shoot the lock. But how do I do that. It looks easy enough in the films. He stood back a little, took aim at the lock, then thought, I might miss, better place the gun against the lock. He wasn't holding it properly and the kick back hurt his shoulder.

The door opened easily and he quickly flipped the light switch just inside the door. Remy was on the bed with the intruder lying on top of her. She was naked from the waist and he had his trousers around his ankles. He looked up in surprise and shock at the gunshot. Remy saw her chance and heaved him off her and he fell to the floor face down. She jumped up and stood on his back. Holding on to the bed she began to kick him with the heel of her foot. Stamping on him with all her weight.

'Hold it Remy, and you, stay still. Get me something to tie him up. The kettle cord will do. Quickly.' To her credit, she did not wait to get some clothes but grabbed the cord and tied his hands together above his head.

'You hold this while I tie him. Do it like this,' as he placed the gun on his back and held it there. This way you won't miss if you have to shoot him.'

'Hey man, we were just having a bit of fun. Let me go, I won't come back.'

Joe trussed him up tightly with the electric cord, hands behind his back, then leaving his trousers and shorts down around his ankles, tied his legs together with his belt. Then he found Remy's sarong and tied it around her.

'Stay with him while I call emergency. The number was printed on the phone. Keep the gun where it is. I have to go up the hill to get a signal. If he tries to move shoot him. I think that's ok in America.'

He was gratified that the police operator answered quickly but he took a while to explain exactly where they were. 'Tell you what, I have a strong lantern, I will leave it on the top of the hill near where we are parked, the police will see it easily, shining up into the air. It's very powerful.

'By the way, if he tries to run away am I allowed to shoot him?'

'Not really just keep him tied up.'

Drat it, thought Joe as he hung up, I'm not registered to have a gun. Better put it away. No that's too late, they will see the door.

Forty-five minutes later they saw the flashing blue and red lights, the siren wailing as a police car sped down the road toward them. Then a second police car appeared. Joe stood at the door and called them in. Drawing their guns to officers burst into the van and instantly took in the scene.

Remy stood her ground until an officer said, 'It's ok ma'am, we're here. Give me the gun. The other officer yelled, 'Drop that gun. Drop that gun.'

Remy calmly turned around and said, 'Do I give it or drop it?' and with a smile handed it over.

'Well, you certainly have a situation here. Tell us what happened.'

Remy lost her composure, and shouted, 'When Joe was outside this creep came in and tried to rape me.'

'Ok ma'am, cool it, let's talk about it quietly.'

The police decided that they should all go back to the station and give their reports. Both of them could type well so were given computer keyboards. They were told to begin at the beginning and leave out no details. Justice moved swiftly and at the court hearing the next day, the local magistrate committed the alleged rapist for trial in the State Court.

They were about to leave when the county prosecutor asked to see them. He wanted to know how it was that as tourists, they had a firearm, and a fine sporting one at that. He accepted their explanation with the proviso that an officer accompanied them back to the van to show where it was hidden. He went on to say that they had discovered that this alleged rapist was a wanted man as he was implicated in three rape cases. He also has a history of bugging people, usually only misdemeanours but a nuisance all the same. In view of this, and for their sensible action in apprehending him, he was willing to ignore the question of the unregistered gun. 'Just tell the owner to come and collect it from me. By the way, I was very impressed with the statements you made, are you writers or journalists or something?'

Because they had given such full statements and that the accused had practically admitted guilt already, they were told that it probably would not be necessary to appear at another court hearing but that they must be available if the judge decides he wants to see them.

Back at the van Joe said, 'I think we ought to get out of here and start again.' Remy cooked a simple meal of scrambled eggs and they moved further on into the desert. They could have two more days and nights in the desert before topping up water and batteries and be rid of the gray and black water.

They found an ideal camping place. It was well used and set beside a fast-running stream provided an ideal spot. Remy cooked a meal and then Joe noticed that she sank down on her bed as though she was worn out. I think the girl is exhausted thought Joe. Last night's escapade has taken a lot out of her.

He went to her side and said, 'Why don't you turn in? I think you are very tired, emotionally drained, I guess. Get undressed and I'll give you a soothing massage. Just show me which stuff to use.'

'It's the blue one. Give me a minute to get into bed.'

Joe knew a good deal about massage because he had been taught by an old woman in Bangkok where he had lived for a few years. His wife and some of her friends had often asked for his help. He took a fresh bath towel and when he found that she had on a long nighty, suggested she take it off and use the towel to cover herself. He turned around as she did this.

'Do you have a headache?'

'Yes, I feel one coming.'

'OK, we start with the head. Using just the fingertips of both hands he pressed her skull firmly but gently moving from the base to the top and then around the sides and down again. 'Oh, Joe that is so good.' He worked on the neck and shoulders and down each arm. Then up again to the shoulders. He could feel the tension gradually subside.

He pushed the towel down a little and worked on her back and all the way down to the base of the spine. He took an hour to give the complete massage after which Remy congratulated him. 'That was very good. Thank you. Now I will sleep well.'

It was still early and Joe went outside and sat beside the stream and watched the moon come up. This trip wasn't working out quite the way he had hoped. A bit of unexpected excitement didn't hurt. That bloke is going to be pretty upset about his gun. Remy is doing well, and she's nice company. But there is something about her he didn't quite understand. She's a capable, intelligent woman and she's far more than a housewife, or a maid. Think of the way she handled that gun. She had a firm grip of it and held it with a certain degree of familiarity. But then her father was a soldier, and her brother, but they would never let her play with their gear.

Come to think of it when she told me the story of her uncle, she said her father pulled out his 45 SAP. Not just his gun but a 45 SAP. Umm, that's the Browning 45 calibre semi-automatic pistol, that much I know about guns. She also knew it was loaded with 7 bullets. 'I've got six left,' her father said.

And when I was shown the gun under this van, she only glanced at it and made a comment, as if she knew all about it. I bet she's been trained in the military and is not saying. What is she doing here with me?

Something I have noticed is that every time she sees a Filipina, she wants to talk to her. That's natural enough but there is something about her and the way she talks to them. She's always very friendly of course, but she is full of questions and later makes lots of notes. Sometimes these conversations end up with an argument with the maid looking quite fearful. What is going on?

Next day they moved into the nearest town to replenish supplies and to recharge the batteries. The motor camp was well serviced with a good ablution block and kitchen. Three of the staff were from the Philippines and Remy was soon engaging them in conversation. That evening after supper Joe said, 'Remy I noticed you like to talk to all the Filipinas we meet.'

'Why should I not?' she said pouting irritably. 'They are my people.'

'Of course, you should but I have been wondering about you.' It was out before he could stop himself and immediately began to regret his outburst.

Remy sat quietly at the table clearly hurt and upset. After ten minutes of quick talking, she appeared mollified and went off to bed. A few minutes later she was sobbing quietly. Joe waited a few minutes hoping she would settle down and sleep but she continued. Clearly, she wanted to make as little noise as possible. He went to her and knelt beside her bed. Taking her head in his arms he tried to soothe her. 'What's the matter? Did I say something?'

She turned her head away and pressed it into the pillow. 'You don't understand. Just don't say anything,' came her muffled voice. 'Go away please. I'm all right.'

He began to massage her head. 'Please don't do that. I'm ok.'

He was awakened next morning by the smell of coffee

and his first thought was, well she can make good coffee. He turned over and stared at her as she bent over the table arranging the breakfast things. She was wearing her usual thin nightdress and with the sun shining through it he could see everything. What beautiful breasts she has, and gorgeous hair that hangs to her shoulders. He lay quietly gazing at her. Wouldn't it be nice if she was always around to get my breakfast but the days of a permanent live-in servant seemed long gone? But she's no servant. Who is she?

She looked up and saw him staring at her. 'You wake up too soon,' and slipped away to dress.

After breakfast he casually said, 'Do you want to talk to your friends here before we go?' He bit his lip. That was unnecessary, you are teasing her.

'We have talked, thank you,' was her rather sharp reply. 'Where do we go today?' He thought about this for a while. Why do I have to tell her what I plan to do, I don't even know myself.

They were soon out on the road and Joe loved the driving. The huge bus handled like a motorcar, steering was so smooth and the automatic gearbox was a dream. The cruise control was a type he had never seen before. He was good for hours at the wheel. His mind constantly went back to the mystery seated beside him. Who is this woman? How was it that she ends up here in my van? Yet it all seemed so innocent enough the way her brother introduced her. Yet he knew enough about the world of espionage and the secret world of government agencies, that nothing was ever as it seems. Always there were forces behind everything working out the will of the powers that be.

But who is this woman? In some respects, she acts like a typical servant and yet her general demeanor suggests something else. Maybe military, an agent of some kind, the product of some special training.

'You are very quiet today,' she commented, 'Are you upset with me?'

'Why do you think I would be upset with you? Those problems we had been beyond your control.

'Can we stop for a while I have something I want to talk about?'

'Never mind, just talk. I can listen and drive.'

'I think you might want to stop when you hear what I am going to say.'

Ah, he thought, I think she's going to come clean. This is going to be interesting. He soon found a suitable park, well off the road and under the shade of some huge trees.

'It's like this sir, I mean Joe. I have been given a special job to do by my government. The government of the Philippines recognizes a very big problem looking at our country. We have had eleven million overseas workers who are on fixed term contracts and they are in 182 countries. They are more widely spread than New Zealanders who have the reputation of being everywhere. They send back about ten billion US$ every year. There are four million of our people in the USA alone.

The problem is that there are too many reports of abuse against these workers. It's happening everywhere. I have already reported back in Malaysia and Singapore and now they have asked me to find out what is happening here.

It turned out that rather than give her diplomatic status it was decided to let her visit as a tourist and travel incognito. They looked at a way to do this and kept a watch on rental companies. Alfredo proved a good agent and came up with his novel idea.

Joe sat and thought about this for a while. She said, 'I'll make some coffee while you think about this.' What to do. If I refuse to cooperate, she will have to take the next bus back to the coast. If I continue, what will happen to my holiday?

'What do they want me to do? Is that my holiday finished?'

'Oh no, you just carry on, go where you want. Everywhere there are Filipinas and I'll just talk to the ones we see. It's like a random check.'

'Tell me, were you supposed to tell me this?'

'Well actually no, I was supposed to keep quiet but I think its best that you know otherwise I am keeping secrets and will have to lie to you all the time, and I don't like that. I have a special phone to give reports so I won't use yours and cost you money.'

'I guess you have a GPS chip too so that they know where you are?'

This time she was embarrassed and mumbled, 'they will know everything.'

There was nothing else for it so he asked her to come clean and tell him all about herself, her training, her real assignment and where all this was going to end. It all came out in a rush. A few months after joining the police she was transferred to a special branch of national security and underwent training in all the skills likely to be needed in this line of work. She was remarkably frank and open about it all. There were courses on weapons training, hand to hand combat, martial arts, secret breaking and entry, lock picking, how to work in absolute silence when checking out a house or a room with a sleeping person being completely unaware of what was going on.

'I am beginning to feel very insecure with you around.'

She came to him and placing her arm around his shoulders said quietly, 'you are quite safe Joe. Please have your holiday and I'll do my job and everything will be all right.'

But how was he going to be able to relax and enjoy a holiday with her doing her job. Maybe I should join her and work for the government too even if it is unofficial.

'How about your boss? Who do you report to and when?'

'Oh, I expect him to meet me somewhere sometime. He's tracking me so he'll find me easily enough. Maybe he'll want to meet you. I was told that should I find a cooperative person then my government will see that you are treated well.'

They set off down the road again Joe's mind all awhirl. What should I do about this? Where will this lead to? Why not send her back on the next bus and call her mother to take over the maid duties? He was enjoying having someone to cook and clean just like the old days and didn't want to give that up. I had a live-in maid for most of my life and so it's nice to go back to that. But having a secret agent do this, surely not.

But things soon settled down because she made no attempt to contact anyone but happily tagged along enjoying the journey. Day after day saw them traversing state after state until they came to New Jersey, with New York City the main objective. They found a campsite on the outskirts of New York then called a taxi to take them to a hotel in the center of the city. 'Take us to a downtown hotel, not a big expensive one, but a small private one,' instructed Joe.

'I know one that is called Number 36. It's good, not too expensive, funny name though,' giggled their driver, a very large Sikh.

CHAPTER FOUR

Next morning after a breakfast of American pancakes with Canadian maple syrup, Remy said, 'I wonder if you would mind if I left you for a few days while I visit some people here.'

'What kind of people, and in New York, what was she thinking of!

'Are you serious? Do you think I would let you loose in this city on your own? No. Not at all, I'm coming with you. Where do you want to go? Who do you want to see? Why this place?' The questions tumbled out-sudden concern erupting.

Carefully she explained that she understood that there were quite large groups of Filipinas in New York City. Like many other racial groups, they tended to gather together in ghettos. Among them were numbers of illegal immigrants who had for the most part come over the border from Canada. They could be found in all manner of small businesses working illegally and in constant fear of being found out. The problem was that she was not interested in illegal immigrants but in the way they were being treated. But to expose a cruel employer was to expose an unfortunate worker and that would result in deportation.

'Anyway, you're not going there on your own. I'm coming too.' She stood up and came near him, her arms across his shoulders, 'How can I thank you; I'm really scared about this.' He replied with a comforting pat.

They found a campsite on the outskirts of New York then called a taxi to take them to a hotel in the center of the city. 'Take us to a downtown hotel, not a big expensive one, but a small private one,' instructed Joe.

'I know one that is called Number 36. It's good, not too expensive, funny name though,' giggled their driver, a very large Sikh.

The receptionist and porter were Filipinos, and they soon found that all the cleaning staff were women from Manila.' Does Ferdinand Marcos own this hotel,' joked Joe to the porter, as they passed by three Filipina maids chatting in the corridor?

'No, but one of his Chinese friends does.'

They were shown to their rooms and as Joe left Remy he said, 'I'm not teasing you but they'll be plenty of people for you to talk to here.'

They were having a drink at the bar when Joe noticed a couple nearby who was acting a little strangely. The man was about 60 and he was with a young Asian woman. When Remy joined him he said, See those two, I wonder what's wrong with them.

'I've just been talking to her at the checkout. Look what she gave me. It's her phone number, she's very unhappy about something.'

'When can you call her?'

'She'll text me soon, after he's gone out to a poker game.'

An hour later came the text - 'call me 4 my add. He's gone.' this was followed by a phone call when she poured out her troubles. Her husband was a retired marine and they met and married in Manila when she was a pole dancer. They lived in a plush house fully air conditioned and curtained. They had two young maids and he required all of the women in the house to go about naked at all times. This troubled his bride and she wanted out of the relationship. Remy listened carefully then had to say that there was nothing she could do about this. What people do in their own homes was their business and provided the law was not broken there was nothing anyone could do except perhaps provide advice and counseling. It certainly was not within the scope of Remy's brief.

'I met someone like that in Manila,' said Joe. 'He answered my advertisement for a maid and invited me to his house because he had someone who might be suitable. He was a retired American businessman who had 'escaped' to the Philippines and said that he was as far away from his wife and family as possible. The woman whom he called his wife had nursed him in hospital when he was suffering from kidney failure. He invited her home and they lived together as a married couple. But he also insisted that all the women in the household wear nothing but the skimpiest of panties. He had three maids.

'Let's do some sightseeing today, I'm not a good shopper but I'd like to have a look at the shops here,' suggested Joe. So they spent the day walking around up and down the long streets of every conceivable type of shop.

Back at the hotel, they agreed to rest for an hour then meet for dinner. When they met Joe could see that Remy was bursting to tell him something and was distraught that they couldn't get a quiet table where they could talk. All she could say was, 'I've talked to two of the housekeepers. There's a lot going on here.' After the meal they sat on the grass at the edge of Central Park and Remy explained that she had already talked to two women, 'And man, do they have stories! I think nearly everyone is involved in some way.'

'I am going to do something that it is maybe dangerous and a bit stupid. I'm going to see if I can get a date with one of the girls.'

'Get a date, that's not possible, they are not available for that sort of thing. You'll have to pay them. And they won't be able to keep the money, their minders will get it all.'

'Don't worry; I know what I am doing. It's the only way to get along with one and find out what's going on. Promise, I'll behave myself. '

'It's not that Joe, I'm sure you will, but it's dangerous. They might be under drugs, got AIDS, could be anything.'

'We could do a foursome, you and I and two of them. You are the lesbian and I'll be the bloke.'

'How could you ever think of such a thing?'

'No, no, all we will do is to get them away somewhere quiet and private and talk. Leave it to me, I'll fix something up for us.'

Next morning Joe went back to his room after breakfast to wait for the maid. He prepared a note – 'my partner and I want two girls tonight. Pretty and cooperative. Good money. We'll give you twice the going rate – half for you personally.'

He motioned to her to start working and not worry about him working at his desk. After sizing her up, he decided she would be ok. The maid was of average height and size, quite pretty and friendly. Holding his finger to his mouth in a gesture of silence, he handed her the note.

'Shsh sh, just read it,' he whispered. Immediately she began to tremble, her hands shaking as she read. Joe took back the note and wrote, 'When and where?'

She looked up with a look of anguish, as if to say, 'Oh no not again.'

'How much?' The maid looked around fearfully as if afraid someone was listening. It was an odd look. Horrified at the thought yet pleased about the money. Scared though.

'I have to ask the boss,' she whispered.

'That's ok, ask him. But you have to come with me not stay here. I've got a big trailer. Tell the boss I'll pay double.'

Then quietly, 'You'll be all right. We'll look after you.'

'Who is your partner. Is he a big man? Is he white?

'No no, he is a she. A woman. A very nice one.'

'Oh she's a lesbian.

'No not really, I think it's called bisexual, likes men and women.'

Joe held out his phone and said, 'Ask him now.'

She tapped in a number, quite a long one. That's interesting thought Joe, she knows the number, must have run it many times. Her conversation was brief, 'I've got a job for tonight, a good one. He'll pay double and take me to his place. He wants two so Lucy can come too. He wants all night for four hundred dollars. O.K?

Hum thought Joe, who mentioned four hundred dollars. Well I suppose that's ok for them both. But there'll be extra for them. What am I getting into? He met with Remy and told her of the assignment. But she wasn't pleased. 'That'll ruin my special budget. I've only got a thousand.'

'You never mentioned a budget. Why is it called a special?'

'I am allowed to spend a thousand on case like this but there will be many to see. They discussed it together and decided that there were two stories here: both girls will have a different experience.

'I don't like you calling them girls Joe, they are women, albeit young women.'

'In my country its quite acceptable to call women, even old ones, girls. It's friendlier.'

'Ok then so long as you don't think of them as children or just big girls.'

Joe picked the women up in a taxi and took them to the

mobile home. They were surprised that Remy was from the Philippines. Remy made a drink for everyone then began to explain why they wanted to meet them. 'Tonight we will just talk. Don't worry, we will pay the money but we want to talk to you about being here in the USA.'

Donna came from a small, isolated village in the hills of Baguio. A recruitment agent came to her village and signed contracts with several young women. They would be given work in the USA; he would arrange for passports and visas and make all the travel arrangements. There was nothing for them to pay, all the expenses would be taken out of their salaries in the US. They had nothing to worry about, but just sign the contract and let him take their photos.

Six months later, when Donna and her family had given up hope of ever seeing him again, he returned to the village bearing a large plastic envelope in which was a passport (this turned out to be illegal) a USA visa, airline tickets to Denver, one hundred US dollars and a thousand Pesos for expenses to get to Manila. Donna was assured that in the USA her salary would be so great that all these expenses would be paid for in a few months and then she could begin sending money home for the family.

The travel to and entry into the USA went smoothly. Her employer turned out to be a Filipino businessman and set her to work as the office cleaner. His wife was also his secretary and came from Baguio city. At lunchtime on her first day, Donna was taken to a restaurant for lunch then a walk around a large mall nearby. The range of products on sale was mesmerizing and she was intrigued to see the way her employer bought things. There was no money involved but he simply handed over a small plastic card.

Back at the office, Donna waited for a chance to ask her employer about that card. 'Oh would you like one. I'll ask my husband to get one for you.'

A few days later he called her into his office and handed over a small card with her name on it. The sound of the name was appealing – Visa. The visa was the wonderful thing that got her into the USA and she thought that these two things were somehow connected. She was after all, from a remote village and never spent any time in a city. At the first chance she was off to the mall with her employer who encouraged her to buy all the things she had always wanted. She soon bought things she had only dreamed of having like luxurious underwear, new shoes, a handbag and new jeans.

Next day, one of the office girls took her shopping and she was soon in possession of a new wardrobe of not just jeans and tee shirts, but her very first skirt and blouse.

A few weeks later, her boss called her in and said, 'I have your Visa bill here. Its' quite large. How are you going to pay it?'

'Pay it! I've already paid for my visa.'

'No, no, not that one, the small card one. Now you have to pay for all things you have bought.' He then went on to explain how the credit card system worked. The math was frightening. It would take her five months to pay off the cost of coming to the USA, then another $900 on the Visa account. 'Go away and think about it.'

Think she did. What could she do other than ask her boss to pay it and she would work off the bill? He immediately told her to move into a room on the ground floor and handing over the keys said 'This is your room. No one else will sleep there, only you.' That was an improvement. It had a large comfortable bed and she had been sharing a small room with four others sleeping on traditional mats on the floor. This was in an apartment block that was next door to her employer's home. It was the first time she had ever had a room to herself. Never in her life had she slept alone. There was always a sibling or a cousin with her. At first, she felt very happy then within minutes, a feeling loneliness swept over her. Alone in a new and strange country. It was so quiet. She lay still and listened. Nothing. No people, no dogs, no roosters, no night birds. Later that evening there was a tap on her door, it was the boss, asking if he could come in for a talk. He began to explain that there was a way she could pay off the Visa bill and also her other expenses. 'There is a man I know who would love to meet you and if you are nice to him, maybe he will help you.'

'But what would I have to do for the money?'

'Don't worry, when you meet him he will explain everything to you.'

In halting English, she tearfully told of the way he seduced her insisting that he visits her twice a week. She admitted that he was very kind and gentle and in three months he had cleared her bill as well as giving her a few small presents. As soon as her Visa card and immigration expenses had been cleared, she took a job at the hotel. But she was still bound to her first employer. One day he explained to her that her Philippine passport was a forgery and therefore her USA visa was illegal. If the authorities discovered this, she would be sent home. But if she continued to 'work' for him, he would protect her and not report her to the Department of Immigration and Deportation. She was required 'to see' one man per week.

Lucy was becoming agitated. 'Ok, so now it's your turn,' said Remy.

'I'm the same as her,' she whispered. 'Just the same.'

Lucy's English was not as good as Donnas so she used Tagalog. When she had finished Remy said, 'Her experience was indeed almost exactly the same in almost every detail from the recruitment, the Visa card trick to her present situation.'

'He's doing it all the time, we know lots of girls like us,' said Donna.

A few minutes later there was another text 'Please call me again. I have a story.' Remy called and was given the name and address of another young woman who had a bad experience in the Middle East. Her name was Amelia. Within 30 minutes of being contacted Amelia was at the hotel lobby only too glad to pour out her story. Not that anything could be done for her now, as it was all in the past but nevertheless they were interested in what she had to say.

After graduating with an economics degree, Amelia, 23, decided that she would find a job overseas. She knew that neither her parents nor eight siblings would be happy about her doing this so she quietly contacted an agency and soon secured a job in Kuwait. Secretly she prepared herself and took off without saying goodbye or telling anyone, not even her closest friends let alone the family.

Later her eldest sister said that seeing she was the brightest one in the family, they certainly would have helped her continue her studies and perhaps become a lawyer.

Within a few days of being in Kuwait she became upset with herself for not letting her family know what she had done. Unfortunately, had she landed a job as maid to three children of a drug distributor and within a month of her being there, he was forced to go into hiding because the authorities were taking an interest in him.

He was so afraid that his wife might spill the beans, he took her with him. They locked the maid and three children in their 7th floor luxury apartment and left without disclosing where they were going. Their plan was to visit the children once a month and instructed the maid that she was not to leave the building or contact anyone. She couldn't leave anyway as they had not left her with a set of keys.

After a couple of weeks, Amelia was suffering from cracked heels and needed some special moisturizing cream. She searched high and low for the keys and finally found them cleverly hidden behind some shelves.

A message came to her saying that because her boss could not go to the bank for fear of being discovered, they were unable to pay her but there was plenty of food in the deep freeze. The keys enabled her to get to the basement of the building where there was a small store. When the Kuwaiti owner heard her story, he was very sympathetic and promised to help. He would arrange for her to escape from the building and go the Philippine Embassy. A few days later, when the children were asleep Amelia went down to the shop and the owner called a taxi. He checked with Amelia that the children were safe and not in danger of touching such things as electrical appliances. He promised that his wife would look in on them. He instructed the taxi to take her to the embassy and return to him with a report.

Amelia did not like the look of the taxi driver so she managed to get a cellophane bag and hid it in her clothing. Her plan was to attempt to suffocate the driver if he did not do as instructed. She would be sitting behind him so it was a simple matter to pull a bag over his head.

The storekeeper took a large cardboard box and covered Amelia with it so that it looked as though the taxi was conveying a large carton.

She was duly delivered to the embassy without incident. The taxi then reported to the storekeeper who then phoned the Kuwaiti authorities to come and take care of the three children who were aged 2, 4 and 6 years.

The embassy officials were kind and understanding. They put Amelia in a room with eight other women who had been ill-treated or abused by their Kuwaiti employers.

A month later a court case was held and during this her employer winked at her. His wife saw this and they had a furious row. Amelia could not understand this because they had both been kind to her and not given her any problems during the first month. The embassy paid for her ticket home taking the money from what was owed to her.

Amelia still has hopes of marrying and having a family. But she realizes that she wasted several important years of her life when she should have settled down and now it may be too late. Perhaps in the USA there is still has hope for a better future.

'But my family has been a bit unlucky with overseas jobs,' she lamented. 'My sister Mary was a schoolteacher and got a job in Singapore. She is very small, not much more than 40 kilos and has always been sickly and certainly not athletic.'

An agent in Manila soon found her a job but the family were not happy. Especially mother. She knew Mary could not work very hard. She would come home from a day's teaching and fall exhausted on the bed. Maybe because we come from a big family, we have had to fight for everything we have, I think we are all like that. Anyway, Mary signed up for the job and took the papers home. Mum cried; Dad blew up. All the kids gathered around him, at the same time, excited for her but a bit worried. One sister had gone to New Zealand and was home on leave. She tried to persuade him not to go. 'It will be much harder than you expect, 99% of all the girls who go away find it to be like that.'

When the time came to leave for Singapore the whole family saw her off at the Manila airport. We were all crying.

Her Singapore family welcomed her at the airport and proudly showed her a single room in their four-bedroom apartment. That in itself was significant as many maids sleep in tiny rooms almost like closets. They gave her a packet of instant noodles for supper and told her start work next morning at 5.30. That was no problem as it would be about sunrise and she was used to that. 'Clean the kitchen, make the beds, wash all the floors then I will show you how the laundry works,' said her boss.

After laundry came the ironing, then prepare the food for the evening meal. She ate with the children, bathed them and put them to bed.

She had to be awake at all times when the children were up spending as much time as possible with them speaking English. The grandmother did all the cooking and was constantly telling her to hurry up. Mary also had to do the dishes. By 9 pm she was exhausted. It was the same every day.

After six weeks the mother took pity on her realizing that the girl did not have the strength to do the work. The agent insisted on being paid and her sister in New Zealand sent Ps60,000 and thus freed her from her obligations.

After a long discussion Joe declared that perhaps all he could do was to give the employer a good fright that perhaps would make life for her countrywoman a little easier. They took a train into the city then stood on a curb watching out for a taxi driven by a Filipino. This was not easy at all. There were Indians of all descriptions, South Americans, and not a white face among them let alone a Filipino. There was nothing else to do but to take a cab to a taxi depot and ask a dispatcher to locate one. There were a few mechanics around but none could speak English. The dispatcher sat in a cramped office yelling into several phones almost without a break.

'Whaddawant? There's a cab over there,' waving a pudgy hand.

'Please call me a Filipino driver.'

'A what?'

'A Filipino, someone from the Philippines, we have a language problem.'

'Naw, get out of here, no Philippines here, too much illegal.'

They took a cab to another depot and lo and behold the dispatcher was a Filipino. 'After you finish work can we talk to you, have dinner?'

They met up in a rough canteen nearby. They were lucky he agreed to meet because he looked very suspiciously at them, as though he feared he was in trouble himself. After strenuously assuring him that he was ok, Remy fired off in rapid Tagalog her concern for her people here in this great city, that like a magnet, had drawn so many into itself. He nodded away all too knowingly, he knew what was going on.

An hour later they had all the addresses needed, but he gave them only after obtaining an assurance they would not try to visit them at night. But they knew that night was the best time, besides if it is safe enough for Filipinas to live there it was safe for them to visit.

A cab dropped them off in a street of old brown stone houses that had once been tidy places in a respectable street. There were a few tiny gardens set between the house and the footpath. Many of the trees had been hacked to death by people looking for wood to heat their winter fires. It clearly had no garbage disposable system, at least not a regular one. The driver pointed to a four-storey building and then flourished his hand downwards as if to say, look in the basement.

A very large Puerto Rican appeared at the door asked them in Spanish what they wanted. Remy's Spanish was reasonable and told him of her Filipino friends. He waved them down the passage staring intently at them. Remy knocked on a door but the fat man motioned them to open up and go inside. It was only the size of a double bedroom but laid out on the floor were a dozen sleeping mats. There was no furniture and a series of nails held clothes of all descriptions, and plastic shopping bags and holdalls that contained peoples' possessions.

Four young women were asleep on their mats. Remy began to speak but Joe hurriedly shushed her whispering that he would like to look around. That didn't take long. Suddenly one of them looked up at them timidly and said, 'Yes, what do you want. Sorry we are pulling here.' They took pull to mean full. Remy squatted down on an empty mat and motioned for Joe to do the same. Then she began to talk. It took a while for the girl's story to come out. Within minutes the other three woke up and joined in. Sixteen women shared the room, these four were on night shift so slept during the day. Their beds would be taken by others after 10 pm.

Remy went into a long explanation of her visit and after the young women could see her genuine concern for them, they relaxed a little and began to tell their stories. But that was not until Joe had shown his passport and explained why he had come. Their stories were practically all the same. They had got into either Canada or the USA on visitor's visas and came to New York for work. They were all overstays by years. They had no social security numbers, no documentation whatsoever.

'How can you live here without documents? What about a job? And the doctor?' Joe wanted to know if this was the kind of life that they had expected in America. Living in constant fear of government officials tracking them down and asking awkward questions, skittishly glancing up and down like wild animals in the forest.

Remy touched Joe on the shoulder and said, 'I don't think that is very helpful just now. Leave that.'

'There are always people to help us. If you pay you can get anything. Just like we pay at home for our papers, we pay here too.'

This was very interesting and Remy wanted to know more about that. How much did the passport cost? They needed medical certificates, education qualifications, work testimonials, so many things they needed. How did they get them? But the answer was the same, you can get everything if you pay. 'Please tell me who these people are, where can I find them?' asked Remy.

There was a loud bang on the door and the fat man entered followed by two thugs. They grabbed the two visitors by the arms and pulled them out into the passage. The girls sprang off their mats and tried to pull them back. They were quickly pushed back and the door slammed shut.

The Spanish tirade that followed was not easily understood by Remy but it was clear they were unwelcome visitors. Two more men appeared and they were bundled into an old van. They were pushed to the floor and a heavy thug sat on each of them. Joe tried to remonstrate and got a severe blow to the head that nearly put him out. Remy began to scream but she was quietened very quickly with severe slaps across her face. Her thug pushed her face hard onto the floor. Her chest was crushed by his weight and she began to gasp for breath. The other one yelled something and he moved from her back to sit on her bottom.

Joe recovered enough to begin speaking but he was silenced by a strip of duct tape that was wound around his head and across his mouth. A stupid thought crossed his mind, that's going to hurt when they tear it off, probably pull out my hair.

An hour and a half later they could feel the van bump across a rough field and pull up so suddenly that the thug sitting on Remy rolled onto the floor. Cursing loudly, he got up and sat down heavily on Remy's bottom. She yelled in pain and he slapped her hard across the back of her head.

The door opened and they tied their legs together around the ankles then pulling their arms behind them, tightly tied them together just above the elbows. Joe thought, that is good they've left the hands free and immediately began to think of a way to untie themselves when they had the chance.

They were dragged out of the van and into an old hay barn that stood close to a derelict farmhouse. Joe was thinking, as always very positively, they haven't blindfolded us. They stood them up and one shouted, 'Now you tell what you do,' then pushed them backwards onto the hay. Joe fell heavily onto a sharp object hidden under the hay. That's another nice bruise, he thought. I think was a shovel. Does it have a sharp edge?

The fat man who had driven the van then gobbled off something to the others and turning to his captives said, 'Right, you are thinking, thinking,' and motioned to the others to follow him outside. The sun was setting and soon it would be quite dark. Joe wagged his head at Remy and tried to indicate that she should tear off his gag. All he could get out was a muffled gaaaag, gaaaag.

Suddenly she understood and rolled across to his side. After a good deal of wriggling, she was able to get her hands onto the tape and began pulling at it. She got a finger under it just behind his ear and began pulling at it. The hair pulled and it hurt but he tried to ignore it. He nodded his head and she whispered, 'Keep still.' There were several layers and it was very tight. She pushed her finger in further and Joe tried to pull away and downwards but she couldn't hold it. She forced two fingers under the tape then three and began to pull upwards while Joe pulled downwards. It took twenty minutes before the tape came off along with a considerable amount of hair.

Joe lay down exhausted and tried to rest for a minute. Next thing he realized that Remy had moved around so that her arms were touching his hands, He soon had her untied and then she reciprocated. They held a hurried consultation and then looked around the barn. There were piles of hay bales, old farm equipment, rubbish of all descriptions and an old tractor that appeared to be in good condition with a full tank of diesel. It was almost the same as a Deere-McCormack he had driven when working on a farm during school holidays. It had no ignition key and he knew that it was powerful enough to drive right through the barn wall if necessary.

'This is what we do, we try and slip out and steal the van. I don't think there are any other vehicles here Let's hope that the keys are still in it. If not, we'll disable it and use the tractor.'

'I can do that; we'll just take the distributor cap off. Easy.'

'Didn't know you can drive.'

'I can't. Just know a few things.'

It was now almost dark and smoke from the kitchen stove suggested their captors were settling down for the night. Joe went first keeping low as he ran to the van. Remy was close behind. Hallelujah the keys were in the ignition. It started immediately and moving slowly and as quietly as possible with the lights off Joe moved the car down the track to the road about three hundred meters away. They had almost reached the wire gate when there were shouts from the house. Joe put his foot down and burst through the gate snapping the wires with a loud twang and down the road and fast as possible.

They soon came to a small town where there was a used car sale yard beside the main road. 'Let's get rid of this thing here and buy another.' We need an anonymous looking car that won't attract attention and they soon spotted a tidy looking Toyota that didn't look too bad in the dim light. A $100 cash, a few travellers' cheques and the old van and they had a deal. 'You'll find the papers of the old one in the cab,' said Joe as they drove out of the yard.

'I didn't see any papers,' said Remy.

'No neither did I but they will be there somewhere. What we must do now is get back to our van and decide the next move.'

Back in their van, that took five hours to find, they went over the past twenty-four hours again and again. They decided Remy should contact her boss, (he's not my controller, I'm not a spy, he's just the boss.)

To say he was upset was putting it mildly. 'You've got messed up with Immigration and Deportation that's not what you were supposed to do.' That was one of the strange government departments, The Department of Immigration and Deportation and it made it sound as though deporting people was just as big as job as allowing them to immigrate.

'Well, there's no separating illegal immigration and our people,' argued Remy.

'You are supposed to just talk to the women and leave the rest to us.'

'I don't think you understand the situation many of them are in, and how can we help them when they have no legal standing.'

'Just find out all you can and give me your report. And don't get mixed up with anyone else. Go to another place and start again.' Remy sank to the floor and began to weep quietly. Joe let her cry for a bit. But after a few minutes he couldn't stand it any longer so he went to her slid down on the floor and held her in his arms.

After a few minutes she dried her eyes with the back of her hand, stood up and said, 'Thanks Joe, I feel better now.'

'You know that fellow was right, we have to think, and think. What to do now? I don't think they will come after us, they were just protecting their own little business, making money off illegals that have no come back. I wish we had the chance to ask each of those women where they worked and how much they were paid.'

'Not much, I bet,' said Joe. 'I have been thinking, I know a policeman in New Zealand who was in New York on some kind of exchange, I wonder if I contacted him if he could put us in touch with someone here who could help us. The police usually know what is going on even if they aren't doing anything about it. Even if it is just to tell us where to look, maybe not just here either.'

'No, we can't do that. I've been told not to contact any authority, police, no one, not even our diplomats. I am supposed to work quietly with people not knowing about me.

'By the way, why don't you phone Immigration and give them that address, they'll catch a basketful of them in one go.'

'Joe don't. Can't you see? I don't want to get these women into trouble, it's the people who help them get here and then abuse them when they do get here, I want them.'

Joe wasn't satisfied. 'I'm going for a walk, be back in an hour.' But Remy wasn't having any of that and wouldn't be left alone. They discussed the problem at length. How can these lousy landlords be caught and punished without witnesses and how could these witnesses expect to be let off scot-free by the thugs who run these scams? They must be contravening a stack of regulations, like, insufficient bathrooms for the number of tenants. Not a registered boarding house. Too many tenants to a room. Probably several Internal Revenue rules also. I wonder if he issues receipts. It was too funny to contemplate and they both burst out laughing. There is probably a whole street of them. I wonder if they are all Filipinas.

'Sorry, but I'm going for a walk.'

'Don't worry I'll stay in sight of the van.'

As soon as he was out earshot, he dialled the number of his friend in New Zealand. Now that sounds simple enough, but the last time he did this he had to go through all sorts of exchanges of phone companies who had no connection rights. But this time it was easy. Henry had just come off shift and after a few pleasantries in which he expressed great surprise as to where his friend was, they got down to a serious talk.

Joe could feel the excitement of his policeman friend who for two pins would come over and join him. His first grandchild was expected any day and there was no way his family would release him. Anyway, this was not a national problem, this was Interpol territory, and he knew just the man. He had been working with an Indian agent on a similar problem. A huge scam had been unearthed in New York and was traced back to Delhi that is the Old Delhi, not New Delhi.

There in a decrepit old warehouse they found a number of men seated at computers who were able to provide any documentation required. Beginning with birth certificates, marriage certificates, death certificates, divorce papers, doctor's vaccination records, receipts of any kind such utilities showing gas, electricity, water and telephone use. Evidence of monetary support. Sophisticated Photoshop type programs could produce any photos required. Fake bank statements were a grand scam. Relatives would send money to a certain bank in the states, and when enough appeared in the account, a bank statement was printed, and then the money was all sent back to where it came from. Offers of jobs all signed and sealed nicely. These clerks could invent a letter in the correct legal prose for any purpose. They had the largest range of rubber stamps and letterheads imaginable.

The contact he was given in New York wasn't very helpful. He met them the next day and explained that the city was stuffed with people doing all manner of illegal things like what he had just discovered. He explained that there were numerous ghettos of people from all over the third world and they all had their schemes of finding ways to stay on in the USA. They had a team who specialized in rooting out these people but they were overwhelmed with the numbers. No sooner is one lot closed down then another appears around the corner.

That they had found one cut no ice with him, brushing them off saying that his people probably knew about them anyway. But surely their violent behavior and attempt to kidnap them was a case worth looking into. 'Of course, kidnapping is a serious matter and that we put this on the back burner for a while is an indication how busy we are dealing with this sort of case. Well, if you want to pursue this, it probably will take weeks before it is dealt with properly. You are both writers I hear, so give me a full written report that we can use at a later date. But I've got a feeling that your people won't want this to go too far.'

Joe's holiday was rapidly fading away. Suddenly Remy excused herself and went outside clutching her phone so tightly the knuckles were white. She returned after a few minutes her face grey with anger. 'They want me to go home, they've cancelled me,' and burst into tears.

The policemen stood up and said, 'I will leave you now, but here's my card, call me if you need any help of any kind. Don't worry about these people; we will get to them eventually. I'll send you my report and all you will need to do is to sign it as correct and send it back. It will be used later. Both of you should also describe what happened giving all the details you can, they will be most useful, I know you can do that well. Send them to me with mine.'

Joe began to give his address but the officer waved him down saying, 'Don't worry. We know who you are and where to find you,' and left them alone. Now that statement has left Joe flummoxed. He began to wonder how much they knew of him. And her. He knew enough of the way certain government departments kept an eye on people but this was ridiculous. A retired man from innocent little New Zealand. Ah, I suppose it's the girl they know about and they have checked up on me too. And how did that FBI man, since that's who he was, know we were both capable of writing a good report.

Joe sat Remy down and after calming her asked for the details of her phone conversation with her boss. She was ordered to return to Manila immediately and give a full report. He was pleased with everything except the fiasco with the guesthouse manager. Relations with the USA were going through a difficult period and this was not the time to aggravate them over an illegal immigration issue. They had something else in mind for her to do. She was to bring Joe along as they believed he might of some help in the next assignment.

'Just a minute, what about the van, it has to be returned to Los Angeles?'

'He said we have fourteen days when we must report to Philippine Airlines in LAX. They will have our tickets.'

What are you supposed to be doing now?'

'I stay with you and we shall have our holiday as planned. I don't have to do anything else; I've done all they wanted me to do. In a couple of days my boss will meet with us and explain everything. Don't worry about him, he will find us wherever we are. He told me to use my phone once a day and he can track us easily. He wants to do it that way because he can't plan exactly when he will meet us.'

Two days later they had just turned into a camping ground when a police car pulled up behind them. 'I bet that's my boss. Yes, it is.'

'Better invites him in for a coffee.'

'Just call me Rick,' he said shaking Joe's hand. He turned and greeted Remy in Tagalog and asked a few questions concerning her well being. He turned back to Joe and said, 'I hope we've got time for a chat.'

'We need a chat all right. What on earth is going on?'

'Come back in two hours,' Rick called to the policeman, 'And then you can take us to dinner. And bring your boss too.'

While Remy prepared coffee, Rick began his explanation by saying, 'You want to know all that is going on, well it's like this.' He went on to explain that his government is becoming very concerned about the welfare of the large number of Philippine citizens working overseas. These problems have been with us for years but they continue to grow. About 11% of the country's population are now called Overseas Workers, that's about eleven million. The more people the more problems. Some countries were worse than others, like the Arab ones. You know, about 10% of all the workers there actually contact our embassies complaining of mistreatment, unpaid wages and especially sexual abuse.

It's not so bad in this country considering that we have nearly three million here, but that's enough to have some people who are breaking the law. So, Remy has been quietly looking around and picking up valuable information.

'Are you telling me that you set her up to travel with me, or at least you set me up?'

'Well yes we did, but we did it in a natural way that we thought you would be ok with.'

But no one likes being used and Joe had to tell him so. 'Tell me who do you work for? Are you police, or immigration or MI something?'

'No need for that, I just work for a government that is concerned for its people.' He flashed a diplomatic ID and passed over a business card.

'We have people, they are everywhere, as I said we've now got 11% of our population overseas. They sent nearly 16 billion dollars home last year. They are important to our economy but we need to look after them better.'

'Yea well I employed several myself when I was in Hong Kong.'

'We know that sir, that's why we chose you to help us.'

'But that was years ago.'

'Sure, but governments keep records.'

'We have plenty of data from research, it's coming out our ears. What we need are up to date bona fide stories of actual cases, anecdotes that will move people's hearts. You've had a little experience here in America to help you understand our problem but this country is not the main worry. They have laws here that we can appeal to but what we need is information from other countries that are more difficult deal with.

'The government is planning a massive campaign to enlighten the people at home and to challenge the countries involved.'

'But your people are everywhere how are you going to do this?'

'You leave that to us; we want you to go to particular places and meet our people. There are some contract male workers that get a hard time like desert construction workers and some seamen, but we are mainly worried about our women, especially maids and nannies and some bar workers. Many of these young women are so naïve about the world. They come out of small villages and into the big wide world and are soon flummoxed by evil people.

'If you agree, your first assignment is Japan. Remy is needed at home for a couple of months.'

'But what about my holiday? I've got this trailer here and it has to be returned to the West coast.'

'No problem, just finish your holiday then contact our consul in Los Angeles. He'll fix you up with transport to Manila. However, we would like you to start as soon as possible.'

'Ok, give me another three weeks. But what about Remy?'

'Sorry, but Remy must go home next week. We are sending her mother to look after you. She'll be here tomorrow and then Remy can go home.'

That night before sleeping Joe wondered if he was being used, or just being lucky or what? Fancy these people organizing everything behind my back. I don't know whether I like it or not. Yet I suppose it's giving me the chance to do something useful and maybe exciting.

CHAPTER FIVE

Remy was a little tearful at breakfast. She seemed quite upset at leaving Joe and handing over to her mother. He tried to comfort her by assuring her that she was serving the country she loved and had sworn to obey. He would do his part because he had come to love her people. He quietly wondered in his heart if he was beginning to love her too.

Next morning while they waited for Renny to arrive, Remy explained that her mother had nothing whatsoever to do with her work although she did know a little about it. She would simply come and look after him. No need to make contact with other Filipinos and collect stories, continue with your holiday. There was time for the two women to be together for an hour before Remy left, or as she put it, 'hand you over to her.'

Amid floods of tears the two women said goodbye and Remy boarded her plane. Renny turned to Joe and said, 'Now it's my turn. Remember, I was the one who taught Remy to look after a man, so I will look after you.'

They checked out of the hotel and repossessed the trailer. Joe went over all the facilities and then suggested they rest for a while.

The parting was brief because Renny arrived only an hour before Remy was to fly out to the west coast. He would have preferred them to overlap by a day so that the new lady could learn the ropes. He took Renny back to the camper van and let her look around. It took but a few seconds for her to note how the gas top worked and knew instinctively to open a window when she was using it. She calmly went about preparing the evening meal.

While Renny cooked, Joe set the table for two.

'What are you doing? That's my job sir.'

'There is something I must explain. First of all, we eat together like friends not like servant and master and I want you to call me Joe. Don't worry. I'll let you do all the work.

He couldn't tell whether the look on her face was pleasure or disgust was, or maybe misunderstanding. But she very quiet while they ate and Joe finally broke the silence by saying, I think you will do very well,' and, grinning, 'I like the way you cook and I'll let you do all the washing up.'

'Today we are going to a small town near Louisville where there is a man I need to see. He is a modular. Do you know what a modeller is?'

'Well, is I suppose he is a male model, shows men's clothes.'

'No, no, not at all. He makes models. You will be surprised how clever he is.

The GPS led him to the exact address and when Joe rang the doorbell, he was surprised when the door was opened by a Japanese woman, who greeted him first in Japanese, then in halting English said, 'Mr. Peter out, come soon, don't worry.' Behind her another woman appeared who seemed be identical to the first. Her English was much better and repeated the information in perfect English.

'He says you must come and settle into your room, and he will come as soon as he can. His brother has died but he will be back very soon, but don't worry, you are welcome and we have been told to take good care of you and your wife.'

'Thank you, but this lady is not my wife, she's, um, ("What is she?" he thought) well, she's, like, my maid.'

'Oh, not your wife,' and the two of them looked at each other instantly understanding and said, 'ok no problem, everybody get a room.'

They had a quick lively discussion then called, 'Lizbet, come make room for guest two.'

Lizbet appeared and Renny's face brightened, 'Oh hullo, you from the Philippines?'

This was a most unusual household. The house itself was huge with seven *en suite* bedrooms. There was a master bedroom with a walk-in wardrobe the size of a small room, that caused Renny to whisper, 'It's like a shop.' The two Japanese women were identical twins. The only way they could be distinguished was the small pendent they wore around the neck. One was Y for Yuki, and the other K for Kazi.

Later, as it turned out, Mr. Peter had 'married them both.' He explained that he fell in love with one, then discovered there were two of them, couldn't decide what to do so their mother urged him to take them both. Their entire family had been decimated in the Hiroshima Bomb leaving her the only living relative because she was away at the time. Weeks later, when she discovered that she was pregnant, she moved friends who had a secure village in the mountains.

Bill Peters was stationed in Japan for several years when he met the family and fell in love. Later when he arrived home, he described the hilarity of falling in love with one woman, then discovering there were two, and try as he might, he could never tell the difference between them. All their lives these women had played tricks on everyone, teachers, friends, even boyfriends and employers but never their mother. She could tell who, who was. There was no way I could marry one and leave the other, so we agreed I marry Yuki but that Kazi could come and live with us. If I was honest, I could never tell who was in bed with me. I just trusted it was Yuki.' Actually, there is a difference, one speaks English quite well, but because they can imitate each other so well you can never be sure.

But Bill was not due back for several hours so Yuki showed Joe around. 'A large room at the back of the house has the models,' she said leading the way down a passage. Opening a door that had a sign 'Look but don't touch.'

'We all have that trouble with our model railroads.'

'Not railroads,' said Yuki, throwing open the door.

There before Joe, packed from floor to ceiling were dozens and dozens of models of boats and ships of all types and sizes. 'Did Peter make these?'

'Yes of course.'

'It would take a lifetime to build all these.'

'It did, in between the railroad. Come with me.' She led him to another door that opened onto a narrow-covered passage to another large building, about the size of a six-car garage. It was an immense model railroad. He looked over it for a minute then said, 'I think I should wait for Peter to show me this,' and turned back to the house.

Renny was in the kitchen chatting with two young women who were the maids of the house. 'They are sisters from home,' exclaimed Renny, 'they are exactly from my village. I know their family.' Subsequent conversations with them soon revealed that they were very happy with their work. 'The only thing is that we can never go out together as there has to be one on duty all the time. I do the cleaning and laundry and she does the cooking and ironing,' said Lizbet.

'What about the Japanese women? Can you tell them apart? What do you call them?'

'No problem for us sir, we just call them both Ma'am.'

CHAPTER SIX

The Philippine consul was expecting Joe and had his tickets and visa ready for him when he turned up two weeks later. He was a little surprised to be booked business class on Philippine Airlines.

While waiting for his flight he Googled information about the international airport in Manila. Many were the stories at that time of utter chaos with hundreds of returning workers, *balikbayan* they called them, the returning ones. Expect long delays at the immigration queues and hassles with the customs. Arriving at midnight he prepared for the worst. He hurried off the plane only to find passage through the airport formalities was very smooth, 35 minutes from touchdown to the hotel car meeting him. Nowhere in the world is it better than this, he thought, it shows you that you can't believe everything you read on the net. Remy was there to meet him and welcomed him with a very tight hug and a kiss that although brief, was truly passionate.

Next day was the all-important meeting with what had become known between them as 'Remy's people.' Ricardo's smile was broad his welcome warm and friendly and this was equalled by his colleague Immanuel. 'We need to give consideration to what should be investigated in both Japan and the Middle East,' he said as an opening statement. In some countries like Dubai, 80% of the population are foreign workers and that includes a large number of our people.'

'I think we need to look at the entire spread of OFWs around the world,' declared his colleague Immanuel. 'Let's see the stats.' He moved to a digital projector set up on the table. 'Take a look at this.' Up came a plethora of statistics. There were Philippine workers in 135 countries. 'Some like Mongolia had only a few dozen, to Saudi Arabia where at the last count was 1,135,003 and they are just the ones we know about because there could be another half a million illegal ones. Put it another way there are 24 Filipino international schools in Saudi Arabia.

'Look at this report in the Business Mirror. The total number of overseas Filipino workers (OFWs) who worked abroad from April to September 2011 was estimated at 2.2 million, according to the National Statistics Office (NSO). They remitted P156.3 billion for the same period. About half of this number are female.

'Recruitment of foreign workers has become such big business here and scams are being uncovered all the time. They range from Haiti to Honolulu. Sadly, some of these scams have been originated by local people right here.'

Rico took over. 'To begin, we would like you to go to Japan. We have many people there and a great many problems. Some have beautiful jobs, but we are concerned about many of our people. Here are your tickets, no need for a visa for you.'

TO JAPAN

For several years Joe and his wife had corresponded with a lady pen friend in Japan and it suddenly occurred to him that maybe she could put him in touch with suitable contacts. Here was a chance to meet her at last.

The moment had come. He stepped out of the airport area and looked around the crowd that had gathered to meet loved ones, friends or business acquaintances. You will easily recognize me, she had written. I will be wearing a black and white dress, looks like white spots over black, and black tights and carrying a brown handbag. You know I wear glasses. I'm, 154 cm tall. I'll be carrying a dark blue camera bag, black trousers and a khaki jacket, he had said.

They knew each other instantly. He was thinking, do I kiss her or just shake hands. And she was thinking the same.

As he drew near, she held out her hand and he grasped it eagerly. But the look in her eyes said something else. The eyes conveyed a deep message of welcome

From her photos he knew she was very pretty. A beautiful woman with clear wrinkle-free face, chubby cheeks, attractive slightly slanted eyes, strong eyebrows, nice nose and sensuous lips, held upon an elegant neck.

Standing beside her was a fine-looking elderly woman, a typical refined Japanese lady. Dressed in a fashionable deep blue woollen short-sleeved jacket over a white cardigan and black skirt. This was her mother and she smilingly bowed. She was flanked by a handsome young man and a bright-looking teenage girl. This was the family. How honoured he felt that they should all come to meet and welcome him. He was glad that this was not a secret visit but known and open to the family. They all bowed respectfully. He returned their bow in the English way by nodding the head. He wondered if they would understand that for the British, even to their queen, a deep nod of just the head meant total respect. That's what he was instructed to do when he met Queen Elizabeth.

But they were all smiles, the son quickly grabbing his suitcase and daughter politely asking, although giving no chance of refusal, if she could carry his camera bag.

Yuki led him to large blue saloon in the car park. Another smaller car was next to it and Yuki opened the door for the family. 'They will go home in this car and I will take you to the hotel in the big car. But then you will come to our place for a meal.'

Yuki drove to the hotel and on parking by the front door a porter opened the door, bowing a welcome. A second porter went to the booth and pulled out his suitcase. This was a young woman who managed the 20 kg. bag with aplomb. Within three minutes the receptionist had handed the key to the porter and invited him to go to his room. The young lady looked about 16 but was probably 21 and instead of using the wheels insisted on carrying the bag along the corridor.

It was a western room and this surprised him a little as he expected it to be Japanese style with a futon on the floor. Like so many modern Japanese hotels, his room was quite small but well-furnished and equipped with all that he needed. He noticed that the porter was well trained in that she placed the suitcase on the proper stand, handle facing outwards for easy opening. In his experience there weren't many porters who did this. He felt in his pocket for tip but Yuki stopped him saying she would pay.

'You are welcome sir, have a pleasant stay in our hotel,' and with a deep bow, the porter left the room closing the door quietly behind her.

'Here we are at last.' And with a beaming smile held out his arms and said, 'Come, give me one of those hugs you are always writing about.'

'Do you want a kiss too,' she asked coyly. He took her in his arms and hugged tightly.

'What time is dinner?'

'It's now, as soon as we get home.'

'How far to your place?'

'About twenty minutes. I'm sorry but we must go.'

Home was actually in a temple that the family had cared for many years, generations actually. It was a fine old building and the living quarters were a mixture of the traditional and modern, quite adequate.

A meal was set out on a low table. The chairs, comfortably furnished, consisted of a back and a seat with no legs. A bowl of miso soup for each, two plates of vegetables, tempura – deep-fried prawns, a meat dish of some description and a large bowl of rice.

The son gestured to the table and said, 'Please take a seat. Let's eat.' He looked at her as if to say aren't you going to eat with us?

She understood the look and said, 'Please you eat first, you are our guest. He sat down folding his legs easily thinking, there's a lot for me to learn about these people and their customs.

Yuki and mother kept close by making sure that he ate plenty. The miso was so light yet delicious and he tried to identify the taste. All the food was delicious, all fresh and nothing processed. He thought, this is good food, no wonder these people look so healthy and not fat.

Finishing with a cup of green tea that complemented the meal perfectly, he rose from the table and bowed to the mother in recognition of her good work. She smiled and returned the bow.

'Now I will take you back to your hotel. My son will come too as is it getting late. He will drive.'

On arrival at the hotel, he asked if she wanted to come in but Yuki said, 'Its' late, I will pick you up tomorrow at nine.' They didn't shake hands, rather he squeezed her affectionately and whispered that he would see her tomorrow.

He showered and was in bed in a matter of minutes. But he couldn't sleep. I'm too excited to sleep, he thought, and picked up the hotel information package. They had a gymnasium but it didn't give the opening hours. He called reception and asked about it. He was told by a young lady with a charming voice that 'sorry sir, the gym I closed but the massage lady is still here. She's here all night. Would you like her to come? If you are tired sir, she will relax you for a good sleep.' That sounded good so he agreed.

A few minutes later there was a light knock on the door and there stood a beautiful lady of about 45 clad in a spotless white uniform coat. 'Massage sir?'

'Sorry sir, no speak English. Dress, down, sleep, you powder, oil.' pointing to the bed. Although the language was all wrong, he knew what she meant. Undress and lie down and did he want her to use powder or oil. He removed the bathrobe and pajama top and lay face down on the bed and said, 'oil please.'

He lay down and closed his eyes thinking that he was tired after an early start that day and travelling all the way from Manila via Hong Kong and wondered what it would be like to actually go to sleep during a massage. 'Relax,' she said. And relax he did. But he noticed that she took her time, arranging her bottles and cloths. He heard a rustle of clothing but took no notice and tried to sleep.

Then there was a tickle as she poured a pool of oil onto his back. After rubbing her hands in it she began to massage the feet. That felt good. Her fingers were strong yet at the same time gentle. Squeezing and pressuring toe after toe then the whole foot then up the lower legs, working on the calf muscles. He dozed. He felt her hands on the backs of his thighs running right up to the top. The pressure increased and was almost painful. This is doing me good he thought.

After sitting for hours in the plane her treatment of the buttock muscles was most welcome. Pressing and pulling they soon felt relaxed. Then she moved up from the small of his back and all the way to the neck. Her long fluid movements up and down from waist to neck were relaxing and he began to feel drowsy.

After a few minutes he felt a light tapping on his shoulder and 'turn.' He turned over and she said, 'velly hansum.'

He looked at her in astonishment. She was naked. Apparently, under her white coat there were no underclothes. He had had his eyes shut for the entire back massage. But he had to admit she was a very beautiful woman. Not young but still very attractive. Quite slim. The first thing he noticed was her breasts. They were quite small, pert little virgin things that stood out proudly. Pink nipples fully extended.

'What do you think you are doing. Get dressed. All I want is a proper massage.' She quickly turned crying, 'vely soly, vely soly,' and quickly dressed.

Pouring more oil onto his stomach she said, poking him, 'vely good not fat.' He supposed she often had fat men to massage. Men with stomachs like a heavily pregnant woman. 'Uu look ok.' She had poured oil onto the flat of his abdomen and it hadn't run off but pooled in the hollow. Then she massaged the abdomen, strong circular strokes that he knew were the right ones for there

Half an hour later she was finished and Joe felt refreshed and wide awake. Picking up her things, she gratefully acknowledged the tip he handed her and left the room. At the door she turned and said, 'Tomollow ok?' And quietly closed the door. He lay down and was asleep in minutes.

Yuki picked him at 9 as promised. 'There are things you must see and know here in Odarawa. We have a special castle, it used to be the biggest in the world, but they have rebuilt it – but it is still very nice. First, we will go to Machikado, it's a very special place where you can find many of our food like boiled fish paste, pickles, sweets, and salty squid, as well as wood mosaic. In fact, our government has asked us to always bring our visitors there so that they can learn about our people.

Later we will go to the sea because this is a fishing port and you can see all kinds of fish there – more than 200 kinds of fish in our city. Then we go to the Kamaboko factory.'

'What's that? Is it a new kind of motorcycle?'

'Don't be daft; it's our famous fish paste. They stick the paste onto a piece of wood and make a nice attractive package. It's very famous.'

'After that we will go to the 500 temples. It's got over 500 Buddhist statues and was made over 500 years ago.'

'I thought you were a Taoist.'

'Oh yes we are Taoists but we respect Buddha too, at least a little bit.'

'Then if there is time before lunch, we will go to the zoo museum'

'I've read about that, it's the Museum of Natural History.'

They had lunch at a tiny restaurant jammed between two commercial buildings. It was only 3 meters wide and about 8 deep. It was run by an elderly couple and their teenage granddaughter and they served only one dish, a local favourite – sea bream on a bed of rice. There were three tables seating six each that were just high enough to put your feet under while seated on a mat. They were the first there and were asked to sit at the end near the back wall. Within minutes the place was packed with office workers on their lunch break.

The young woman served them swiftly but she was a bit naughty in that her skirt was very short and showed her underwear when she bowed down to serve. 'This is a very funny family,' whispered Yuki, 'I've heard the old people argue about the girl. He likes the skirt because the male customers like it, but the woman thinks it disgusting.'

They spent the afternoon driving around the district and

along the waterfront inspecting the many fishing vessels.

'I have something to do at the temple so I will take you to the hotel and pick you up at 5 o'clock. Tonight, we will visit my uncle. You will like him. He's very old and rich and he lives in a very big house. We will eat there because he has his own cook and maid. The cook is Chinese from the Philippines but has lived in Japan for many years. The maid lives in and has worked in his house for about 10 years. Not many people here have their own foreign cook and maid.'

The meal was memorable. Yuki took over hostess duties and served the meal, kneeling between the two men keeping the food in the many dishes within reach and the tiny sake cups full.

Back at the hotel Joe asked her to sit and listen to him. He had no chance of explaining the purpose of his visit and he pondered how to explain the real reason without offending her. He had heard how she had explained to her uncle that he had travelled all the way from New Zealand just to see her. He called for drinks then carefully explained that after spending another day sightseeing, he had to get on to his job.

Her response was immediate and positive. 'Oh, I know people who can help you. I'll make some arrangements tonight.'

After a day of sightseeing, they met the uncle at a restaurant in the setting of a Japanese garden. Their standard low table was set beside a pond with large colourful Koi goldfish. The meal was to be a traditional Japanese dinner that could, according to his guidebook, consists of anywhere from 6 to 15 different kinds of food. Joe actually lost count of the great variety of food served that ranged from a simple cup of tea to marinated 'food from the mountains.' He tried not to notice the cost but it was about $150.00 each. The hostess wearing a beautiful brightly coloured silk kimono knelt between Joe and uncle and kept the tiny cups of sake full.

After the meal they retired to a small alcove when Yuki explained to her uncle what Joe required. He listened carefully and thought for a few minutes before answering. 'The great problem is that the people whom you look for are employed by underground criminals, the *yakuza*. Oh, they are not hidden that you cannot see them, but what they do is out of sight. They protect themselves from outsiders, and all of us', waving his hands around, 'are on the outside. I need to think about this and talk to some friends.'

Two days later, Yuki called to say that Uncle was ready to help them. They were to meet for a sushi lunch downtown. The street was crowded, a sea of dark heads, the men all in black and many of the women sporting an assortment of browns, broken by the occasional taxi nosing its way down the busy thoroughfare. They would have the sushi lunch in the red-light district. Sushi had become a common snack at home but he soon discovered that in Japan, it was a costly and very special meal. The menus showed the cheapest meal to be about $35 and the most expensive over $80. Joe asked Uncle to order but he demurred to Yuki saying, 'It's the woman's job today to choose the lunch.' That's clever, thought Joe, Yuki will know where to pitch the cost of this meal.

The meal over, Uncle handed Yuki a folded piece of paper, not with just a straight fold, but cleverly folded to form a telephone. 'Take this and see what you can find. My friend understands and he will help you but be careful to follow his instructions properly.'

Yuki deftly refolded the paper into a cell phone, saying 'We love our keitai. That means phonetic.' There were three numbers to call. 'I will talk to these people tonight so let's meet at ten for coffee at your hotel.'

'Now there is something that you must know,' said Uncle, 'These yakuza cannot be meddled with. Talk to me first before you do anything.' The grave looks on his face said everything. Nothing inscrutable about this man, thought Joe, he's worried.

After coffee next morning Yuki suggested they take a walk while they discussed what to do. She had the names of three establishments that employed foreigners. The problem was that they were not free to contact the Filipina direct, it had to be done within the business. The only way Joe could speak to a woman was to hire her. There were several ways of doing this depending on the service they were offering. Uncle liked to go to a certain bar in the red-light district. He says it's not a bad place but it is his regular watering hole. There are several foreigners there but he doesn't know where they come from.

That evening, Uncle and Joe went out for a drink. There were several streets of bars, clubs and small shops of every description as well as the ubiquitous noisy pachinko parlours all brightly lit with flamboyant signage. They went down a short dark alley into another area of what seemed to be shops without front window displays. Although it wasn't obvious to a stranger this was the place where many hostess bars, host, hotels, shops, restaurants, and nightclubs are located and is called the Sleepless Town. Yuki called it the Neon-gai and he could see why. Each establishment had large neon signs advertising their business some with occasional English words such as 'Best Here' or 'Liking Much.' Like the rest of Japan, it is quite safe to walk around the streets at night.

As they walked Uncle tried to explain where they were. Although he never spoke a word of English when he was with the others, being on his own, as it often happens with language learners, he felt free to try his English. There was no one around who knew him and thus would cause him to be embarrassed. He stuttered out his words breathing deeply between phrases. 'Here many places, good, bad, not bad,' he said. 'You can happy here no problem. Many nice women, bad women, good food, bad food. Drinking can. Much money good. My place good. Other place bad.'

Uncle pushed open the door of a more somberly lit place between something called 'Soapsuds' and 'Healthy fashion' to be greeted by a tall heavy man, obviously the one in charge of security. He was smartly dressed in a dark suit and greeting Uncle like an old friend opened another door into a brightly lit hallway. Two pretty kimono-clad women of uncertain age bowed low in greeting, saying in unison *'dou itashimashite'* several times. They then opened double doors that led into a small bar that had about a dozen stools against the bar and a few two-seater settees. They were the first customers of the evening. A young man stood behind the bar and bowed in greeting. Standing around the room were several young Asian women whom Joe could tell were not Japanese. He quickly sized them all up deciding that three were Thai, two were Indonesians and four from the Philippines. Apart from their facial features they each had something else that identified them. It was a small badge of a Japanese flag and their country of birth. Joe had always prided himself in the way he could recognize different Asian nationalities. The management of this place clearly wanted customers to know that they were to be served by exotic foreign girls.

A Thai girl approached Uncle and showed him a seat. They appeared to know each other. Joe smiled at the Filipinas and the four approached him holding out their hands in greeting. 'Who would you like to drink with?' asked one.

'You are all so beautiful, how can I decide.'

'Oh, that's easy,' said the tallest, 'buy us all a drink.'

Joe quickly scanned their faces and decided on the one who looked the least relaxed and happy. 'May I choose you,' he asked.

'Thank you, I'm Melissa.' He led her to a settee in the quietest corner of the room.

'I'm surprised how small this place is,' said Joe, attempting to open a conversation.

Melissa smiled and said, 'There's more to this place than this,' pointing to the stairs. 'Up there we have a dining room and other rooms. Do you want to see?'

'No, later, let's have a drink first. It's so hot outside I am very thirsty. Do you have a spiritza, just a mix of white wine and lemonade?'

'This is a very nice place,' said Joe, hoping it would be a leading statement. 'But as soon as I saw you, I thought that you didn't look very happy. Are you feeling ok?'

She gave him a startled look, 'How did you know?'

'I would like to have a long talk with you about something, where can we go?'

'For talking, right here.'

'Tell me about your job here.'

'I am hostess. Serving you drinks, whatever you want.'

'Do you go upstairs or go outside too?'

'Yes, for dinner, we go upstairs and I am your waitress, but I don't go outside from here with you. This is a good place. We are all good people here.'

'Would you be able to help me do a survey of Filipina workers here in this district. Don't worry, I am not government, I am a writer and I want to know about your life here and the lives of other OFWs.'

Melissa didn't like the sound of that and it took a while for Joe to convince her that he was genuine. The fact that he was with Uncle helped because he was known to them all. Joe asked her about her family back home and why it was that she was working in Japan. It was a familiar story. The large family needed help and being the eldest, she felt it was her duty to work and support her six siblings with their school fees. In two years, she had almost enough saved for their entire family to finish their basic education.

'That's wonderful, but what about the next stage, should some go to university?"

'Yes, some should, but I don't even want to think about that just now.'

Because accommodation and meals were provided, plus work clothes, Melissa lived off her tips and saved all the salaries. The nine girls shared two rooms, sleeping on traditional futon on tatami mats on the floor.

He discovered that although Melissa was treated well by her employers, she was never allowed a day off. It was six ten hour shifts a week in the bar and one doing the house cleaning in the senior mamasan's flat. Her salary was paid according to the contract, never failing to be paid into her bank account at the end of each month. They had set up Internet banking for her so she could send money home or save it as she wished.

It was clear to Joe that this 22-year-old was simply tired out. Not that the work was hard, in fact it was often quite boring with no customers at all some nights. But the girls were required to always be standing and instantly alert to any person who came through the door. They began work at 4 pm and finished at 2 am. The bar was supposed to close at midnight but a regular gift to the authorities enabled them to stay open another couple of hours if necessary. Reporting for work at midday when they cleaned and polished the bar and dining room really meant they were on duty for 14 hours. They were never allowed to go out of the building alone but always in groups of three or four and always with one of the mamsams as chaperone.

Joe summed up their experience as being well paid and cared for as far as food and clothing were concerned. Personal safety was never as issue, and never a requirement to undertake questionable duties. It was just that they were overworked, not exactly a salubrious lifestyle but with always the danger of alcoholic poisoning. The women always drank with their customers but it was usually a watered-down version of vodka or sometimes just sweet water. They were paid a basic salary rather than a commission on the drinks they sold, as is the custom in some places.

After an hour or so Joe managed to explain the real purpose of his visit and Melissa was soon giving him the names and phone numbers of people whom she knew were in serious trouble. 'But you can never meet them, always you have to hire them,' she explained, 'and they will cost you a lot of money.'

Next morning Joe texted the Philippines and asked for a special budget for his 'research'. He was surprised, not just at the answer but how quickly it came: 'We will pay all reasonable expenses.'

He waited until midday before texting the contacts and after introducing himself said 'Melissa gave me your number. May I see you tonight? What is your address?' Three answered within minutes. All were positive and gave details of the places where they worked.

He chose Juliet. Her address was easy to find as it was directly opposite Uncle's favourite bar. It was called 'Warm Welcome to Everyone.' This meant it wasn't one of those places that did not admit foreigners. With Uncle's approval, he went along at 9 pm and was welcomed by the usual tough-looking front door guard. A middle-aged woman was seated at a reception desk and after a welcome greeted him in perfect English. 'We have very capable and very nice massage ladies here and they will service you very well,' she said. 'They can do anything, Shiatsu, Swedish, everything. Better you take two hours because discount for that. Eighty dollars.'

'I would like to see Juliet because my friend says she is very good, not hurt too much.'

'Of course, Juliet you may. Please have a seat,' and she swiftly phoned for her to come.

Within seconds a young Filipina woman appeared at the door and moved forward holding out her hand. 'You are Joe? Welcome sir. Please come with me,' and bowing slightly to the receptionist led him away. They went down a long corridor with rooms on each side, some with the doors open. Each appeared to be decorated differently mostly in pastel colours. A blue room had blue furnishings, curtains and bed covers and a blue spa bath. Red was all red. Pink was definitely pink all over. Joe paused at one coloured mauve. 'Not this one,' said Juliet, 'I don't like it. Mine is the yellow one.'

At the end of the corridor Juliet opened the door of a room that was a delicate yellow.' At first glance Joe didn't like it but soon became accustomed to the way it made the skin glow. Juliet's light brown skin became a gentle white with a faint tinge of yellow, not that it made her look jaundiced, but quite attractive. Her white uniform, a white blouse and knee length skirt took on a yellow tinge.

'Please tell me sir what you would like. I can do anything for you. Shiatsu, Swedish, very strong, very gentle, whatever you like.

Joe took out his notebook and wrote 'Is it ok to talk about anything here?' Juliet looked up in alarm, 'Of course sir. You, we can talk. About anything. No problem. They said you want to talk.'

'Ok, to make it look right, please give me a Swedish

massage and we can talk.'

Juliet gave him a pair of paper shorts and a dressing gown and left him to undress. She returned with two bottles of beer and a teapot and cups asking what he would like to drink. He chose the tea.

'Juliet, did your friend explain why I want to see you?'

'Yes, a little, but I don't properly understand.'

Joe then set about explaining his mission carefully explaining that she wasn't in trouble, and that her name or place would never be disclosed unless she gave permission. He just wanted factual stories of people like herself who were not being treated fairly. If the facts warranted, the appropriate authorities could be alerted but only if she wanted that.

Juliet's case was borderline. In one way she was happy about her experience in Japan but it was not exactly what she was promised or contracted to do. She was a properly trained masseuse and in general that is what she did. However, from time to time her madam asked her to sleep with clients. She was never forced to do so but always was asked first. Sometimes at the end of the massage her madam would phone and ask her to offer the 'special service'. But she was required to go outside to a small hotel for this. Sometimes she did so if she liked the man and earned good tips.

But this was another case of never getting time off, or maybe, one day a month at the most. She had no way of escaping from the hold her employers had on her as they kept her passport and return ticket to the Philippines. Her six-month contract had been extended to one year. 'Physically I am not too tired,' she said, 'because I usually do only one or two massages a shift, and sometimes none. So I can sleep!'

Uncle had asked Joe to contact him after his first

encounter with a Filipina. He was pleased with his report and said he would be there soon to take him to another place. He arrived within a few minutes in his chauffeur driven car and took him to a second address he had been given. He had the driver stop a few meters away while he tried to sum up the place. There was a notice in Japanese stating that they only took in Japanese people, no foreigners. 'You can't go there,' he said, 'unless you have permission.'

'I think I do,' said Joe, 'let's call this number.' Baby from Manila answered, she was expecting his call. Joe asked her to give the phone to her madam and let Uncle speak to her. She agreed, so long as he was uncle's guest.

The two-storey building was jammed in between two office blocks and appeared to be of unpainted wood. Probably would look quite nondescript in the daylight. There were two large neon signs each side of the doorway that lit up the tiny porch, that when they stepped into, found themselves facing a large tough looking character looking every inch the door man and chief chucker-outer. He was dressed in a black suit reminiscent of a Chicago gangster of the 1950s. A sure sign that the yakuza were in control here.

He stared very hard at Joe while Uncle explained that the mamasan was expecting them. He opened the door that led into the reception area. After exchanging business cards with the mamasan, they were taken to a small side room where an attractive young woman, a girl really, probably only just into her teens, served them tea.

Uncle was then called to the receptionist and cashier where he surrendered his credit card and discussed their requirements. He asked for a Japanese masseuse selecting her from a book of photographs and requested Baby for Joe. Before leaving Joe, Uncle placed his finger on his lips as if to say, 'be careful what you talk about here.'

Baby soon appeared. She was truly a beautiful Filipina and taking his hand, led him upstairs to her private room. Joe asked her if she understood why he wanted to see her. 'Yes, I do,' she said, 'but...' Joe waved his hand to quieten her and took out his notebook and wrote 'we can't say much here. Can we meet outside sometime?' She wrote, 'No.'

'Are you very happy here?'

'No, I am not. It's very bad here.'

'What's the problem?'

'No holiday, they force me sex, no money, no go out, no passport.'

'Send me a text about it.'

'Ok. But only from the toilet, all the time they watch me here.'

It was at that moment Joe thought he noticed something flash on the ceiling near a corner. He stood up and looked carefully. There was a tiny camera lens, no bigger than the lens on a phone camera. He unobtrusively checked all four corners and there was one in each.

Uncle's warning suggested that the room was wired for sound, but he had found cameras. In a loud voice he said, 'Thanks for writing down your address and your family's address, I will visit them next month when I go to the Philippines and tell them you are fine. Now give me a massage.'

The massage was done well although having two in one night was a bit hard on his back. Baby suggested him soak in a warm bath while he waited for Uncle because he had taken a hot and cold bath, then a scrub followed by a massage.

Outwardly everything looked quite ok in this establishment but Baby's message indicated otherwise.

Her written statement was enough to work on.

There was one more to visit but Uncle had had enough for one night. That was a pity as he was to be out of town for a few days. He texted the third contact, Rose, and asked her for a time tomorrow. His quick reply was '10 o'clock.'

'Is that am or pm?'

'Anytime.' Apparently, she was in a 24/7 establishment.

Next morning, he handed a taxi driver a card with her address. He blinked and pointed up the road. Joe waved him to proceed. Not 100 meters up the road he stopped and pointed to a building, laughing with either embarrassment or glee, Joe couldn't tell which. He took the money but shook his head as if to warn him.

This place was a real neongai the two outer walls were glass windows of garish neon lights. He nervously pushed opened the door not at all sure that he as a white man was welcome. The usual security guard actually smiled at him and waved him through an open door to the receptionist. Behind her stood a line of about a dozen women who all bowed in unison chanting a greeting. The lady at the desk spoke English and asked him what he wanted. Was it to be a bath, a scrub, or massage or everything?

Joe chose everything thinking that the longest time possible would be best after being assured that he certainly could have Rose for $95.00. After paying cash he was offered tea in an adjoining waiting room. A young woman poured his tea and said, 'I am Rose. I'm pleased to meet you.'

'Are you Rose?' Joe asked stupidly, seeing at once she did not appear to be a Filipina.

'Yes, I Rose, I come from Thailand. Where you come from? This was embarrassing and Joe went back to the reception asking for Rose from Manila.

'Oh, that Rose, very sorry she is busy. You must wait half hour, but this Rose is very good. Very sweet. Good massage, Thai one, very strong.'

'Ok, ok, you wait. The other Rose, she gives you nice drinks. You like beer, sake, tea, anyone?'

Joe slipped her five dollars and she served him cheerfully enough. Her English was very limited and Joe soon found he knew more Thai than she English.

Manila Rose appeared thirty minutes later and led him to her private room. Aged about 25 years, and speaking good English, she was able to converse fluently about her family. Rose was the eldest daughter of five but had two older brothers. One was handicapped and couldn't work and the other was a seaman but seemed to waste all his money. 'He was like that boy in the Bible,' she said, 'you know the one, he wasted all his father's money and had to feed the pigs?'

'Ah, you mean the Prodigal Son. But he did eventually go home and his father forgave him.'

'Yeah, but that hasn't happened yet.'

'Well, maybe you had better pray for him, that he will run away from that life he has.'

'No way can I pray here. It's a bad place. I'm a bad girl.'

'Did Melisa tell you about me, what I am trying to do?'

'Yes, but only a little. What can you do for us?'

Joe felt a little uncomfortable talking so freely and began to look around the room for signs of cameras or microphones. But he knew that without a proper search, he could never be sure of complete privacy. He took out his notebook and tearing out a page wrote 'Can we talk here? Is it ok?'

She looked up, 'Sure we can talk, no problem.'

'Ok then, I want to know about your contract and if everything is ok like what you expected?' Rose shook her head vigorously and began a long tale of how she applied for a job through an agency in Manila. She was advised to get some qualification like a masseuse. Because she knew a little about this from her mother, she soon found a company that would issue a certificate that was good enough for a Japan visa.

The contract was a generous one guaranteeing accommodation, all food and lodging, uniforms, medical care, and a monthly salary of US$750. She would have to pay back $3,000 to the agency for air tickets, visa and agency fees. It would all be paid in three months so at the end of her six-month contract she would have US$1,500. Then a second contract for another six months at $750 meant she would have earned $5,250 in one year. This was so much more than all the family could expect to earn in a year at home.

The problem was that the $750 came from her having to sleep with her clients. 'But I'm lucky,' she said, 'There are many girls here so I only have to service two a day. I was married for a couple of years so it can be very nice if the man is ok. I hear some girls do 4 or 5.'

'How is your health?'

'I am very healthy, they give us good food and there's plenty of time to sleep, but I can't go out because we work every day. I get three days off every month when I need it. But I must stay here. They've got my passport and ticket. But I told you I am a bad girl because, sometimes I like my job.'

Back on the street again Joe looked around for another possible contact. A tout touched his arm, 'Come with me, you will find what you are looking for. We have many beautiful Asian women.'

'How do you know what I am looking for?'

'People like you come here for only one thing. Come I will show you a good place.' Joe didn't like that. But, he thought, I suppose he is right, and followed him. Fifty meters down the street was a traditional house that had no signs outside. This is either quite illegal or very special thought Joe. It was situated on a triangular shaped corner, a good example how the Japanese utilise every inch of space. Stairs to the three stories were attached to the outside of the building. The ground floor comprised a shop selling electronic goods. Joe paused to look at the merchandise and found a very inexpensive cell phone. On impulse he bought it with a SIM card thinking, this might come in handy at some time. His guide pointed to the stairs and told him to go up to the first floor. There he found the receptionist and cashier. A young girl retrieved his shoes and placed them on a wooden rack. It must have been a busy night for there were many shoes. She was dressed in a kimono and looked about 12.

A variety of services were on offer but before choosing one, Joe tried to engage the receptionist in conversation. 'I like Japanese woman very much but I also like other Asian women. Do you have some from the Philippines?'

'The receptionist, a middle-aged woman, immediately stood and bowed and said, 'Of course, you may choose one. I will call the best one. If you want body scrub then better Japanese, if you want massage then Philippines. First you pay the entry price 3,800 yen and then the scrub 4,000, and shiatsu massage 5,000.'

'Just the massage please,' handing over his credit card wondering what his people will think of another 150-dollar charge, after all the others of the evening.

The little shoe girl then escorted him to a small room on the next floor and, bowing low, opened the door calling, *'kokyaku katai'* that Joe found out later meant 'honourable client.'

A Filipina immediately appeared at the door. She had been alerted by the receptionist and greeted Joe by name. 'Hi Joe, I'm Edna. Welcome. Please come in and have a seat.'

Joe decided that he should adopt a different style and allowed Edna to provide the massage first before talking to her. 'I'm tired and I will sleep while you massage.' He said. 'Make it medium strength. But just do thirty minutes then we can have a chat.'

Carefully and quickly, he explained his mission. Edna's reaction was swift. 'I don't want to talk with you.'

Sensing a real problem Joe took out his notebook and asked, 'if you can't talk now, will you speak on the phone?' Edna wrote, 'They have taken my phone, I can't speak.'

'OK, no problem, here is a phone that you can use. Call me tonight or any time and tell me all about yourself. Let me take the number.'

'Please don't call me, they will hear and take it away.'

After assuring her of not bringing trouble to her, Joe left. He had the feeling that although everything looked quite normal and proper, this young woman was not in a good situation. 'Please call me soon,' and took his leave.

It was 2 am by the time Joe was back in his hotel. He was well asleep when his cell phone rang. It was Edna. Struggling to wake up he asked her what was the problem, why call so late in the night? 'Oh, I am very sorry sir, but now everyone is asleep so now I can talk.'

'You appear to be in some sort of trouble, what's the matter?'

'Sir, my employer is very mean. He does not pay me. I cannot rest, no day off. I cannot go out. I am six months here and my contract is expired. My visa too. Expired. I will have trouble soon from the police because I am an over stayer. They try to force me prostitute. They take my phone. No one knows where I am.'

'Now you have a phone so you can call someone.'

'Oh, but the numbers are in my other phone.'

'I want you to text me the name of your employer and your contract number and your agent too. After two days I will come again for a massage.'

CHAPTER SEVEN

Next morning when walking down the street a rather tall man pressed against his side and as Joe tried to move away another appeared on the other side.' Just keep walking',' said the first. Joe stopped and a third man right behind him gave him a gentle push saying, 'walk.'

'Just keep going, we will not hurt you.' After 100 meters they turned into a narrow lane between two traditional houses. There has been only just enough room for them to walk three abreast. They came to a house with a red lantern burning above the door. One rap loudly on the door and it was opened immediately by an elderly man who stood aside and let them enter.

They pushed Joe into a side room and told him to wait. He immediately realised that the yakuza had been alerted to his activities and he began to imagine having to face the ire of the leader. He wondered if he would be an old man with a wispy beard who would glare at him savagely.

After a few minutes a man entered the room and took a seat behind a large desk. He was quite young, maybe 30, well-groomed and certainly very sure of himself. 'We want to know what you are doing here.' He spoke like a well-educated American with a slight intonation that bordered on an English accent.

He could see the surprised look on Joe's face and said, 'Yes I speak English; I was four years in the States and two in England. Now tell me, what do you think you are doing here? We know that you have been troubling some of our foreign women who are here to serve our customers. What are you trying to do?'

'Who are you? Why have you brought me here? I've done nothing wrong.'

'You know who we are.'

Joe's mind was racing. Was it best to fob them off with a story about looking for some lost soul, some woman who has lost touch with her family and he was trying to find her? Or should he come clean and tell them straight what his mission was?

What to do? From his reading he knew there was no way he could fight the yakuza. They probably knew far more about him than he realized. He just didn't know what to say, so he said nothing for a few moments.

'Look, let's not beat about the bush, we know what you said to Baby.'

'But I didn't say anything to Baby.'

'Yes, maybe, but why did you write to her. We could see what you wrote. Look, I've got the paper here,' pulling a small piece of paper from his pocket that Joe instantly recognized as a sheet from his notebook. 'What is the secret? What do you want to talk about? Who are you working for?

'What about Miss Edna? Why did you give her a phone? We saw you give it to the girl.' Joe recalled that when he was with Edna, he never gave microphones or cameras a thought.

What to do? At worst they could chuck me out. But I've brought real trouble to these young women.

He looked at his interviewer and said, 'Your English is so good so I guess I had better explain myself.'

'Of course, my English is good, I suffered learning it for long enough.'

'That's good. Suffered is the right word trying to learn

our language? It's not easy to speak it correctly.'

Joe decided to come clean. Carefully he explained the problem faced by overseas workers. While the government encourages them because they mean a lot to the country, some of them are not treated well. He was looking into this problem on behalf of a special NGO, not the government, he emphasised.' Taking the bull by the horns, Joe went on to suggest to him that perhaps his organisation could help see that the workers' conditions were improved. They could still get their cut whatever it was, but they could force the employers to treat the people civilly and humanely. It would mean better work and service of the people.'

'We don't take kindly to you telling us how to doing our job.'

'I am worried about the young women I have met. Can you assure me that they will be all right, that they won't suffer because of my stupidness? (Joe thought it was better to debase himself.) It is not their fault that I have contacted them. That one called Edna was the one a tout took me too. He met me on the street; it was nothing to do with Edna trying to contact me.'

'We know all about that. Who do you think that tout was? He works for me. We give these women work. They need us. We also help many poor people and when disasters strike, we are the first there to help. Like the great tsunami, we were there even before the government.'

'I have heard about that,' said Joe, 'You even sent a helicopter to Fukushima. But please leave the Philippine women alone. It's their employers that are the problem, not treating them well.'

'I have some advice for you Mr. Joe. You must leave here right away. No more talking to our women.'

'I am booked to leave the day after tomorrow, don't worry

I will be on that flight. But maybe, I will want to have a bath and scrub and possibly a massage. Is that ok?'

'Sure, that's ok, but remember, we will be watching you. When you want something, come to the same spot in the street and our man will take you to a good place.'

Back at the hotel Joe took a look at the small shops in the basement He found one specializing in inexpensive cell phones. Joe decided that a couple of these could come in handy.

The hotel lobby had a variety of newspapers available for guests and Joe's eye caught a piece that described some of the modern problems of Japan.

"Japan continues to be an international hub for the production and trafficking of child pornography. Japan is home to an immense sex industry that includes a wide variety of commercial sex operation models, including themed-brothels, hostess clubs, escort agencies, 'snack' clubs, strip theatres, and street prostitution. Many are owned, controlled, or 'taxed' by the Japanese organized crime network, the yakuza, or increasingly by foreign-based groups such as Korean or Colombian crime networks. Japanese men continue to be a significant source of demand for child sex tourism in Southeast Asia."

It took a long while to get to sleep that night. The more he thought about what he had read in the paper, the more he thought about the need to pursue his newfound work.

Next morning at ten o'clock Joe sauntered up the road near the place where the tout found him. He must have been on the lookout for him because within minutes a voice beside him said, 'You come again. Very good time yesterday? Come I take you to better place.'

Close by was a wooden house, unpainted with a look of decay about it, and the tout pushed open a door with a small sign on it. He led him to a side room where customers waited for the receptionist. It was lined with mirrors and garish paintings of what he took to be ancient royal courtesans. His guide pointed to a padded couch and said, 'Sit and wait for her.'

A young woman, hardly out of school came with tea and biscuits. She knelt on the floor before him and offered the drink. A few minutes later a middle-aged woman clothed in a bright yellow kimono entered and said, 'I am the mamasan, what would you like today?'

'Well, what do you have?'

'We have everything. Bath, scrub, massage, steam, sleeping, everything.'

'I'd like a bath, scrub and massage please.'

'You are waiting here. She will come, but first you pay. Give credit card.'

Reluctantly he handed her a Mastercard hoping that there would not be any funny business. 'Just a minute, how much?'

She reached into a pocket and produced a coloured brochure listing all the services and prices. 'If you want, one hundred dollars for everything. Very nice.'

'OK,' agreed Joe.

Five minutes later a beautiful woman of about 30 entered the room, and bowing low, said, 'Welcome my name is Yuko, come with me Mr. Joe.' He could see immediately that she was a classic beauty. White porcelain-type skin, no sign of a wrinkle, of slight build and a little over five feet.

Joe had first asked for a bath and scrub. He was shown the bath, as big as a swimming pool with a clear plastic divider separating the men and women. Yuko showed him where to take a shower soaping himself thoroughly then step into the bath. He hesitated and Yuko said, never mind I will do it.' She began to unbutton his shirt while he unzipped his trousers. Taking him by the hand she pushed him into a shower cubicle and turned on the water, handing him a large cake of soap. Averting her face, she closed the shower door saying, 'soap, much soap.' What glorious soap it was. He had never seen such a lather.

After rinsing off he cracked open the shower door. Yuko was there and taking him by the hand led him to the bath. It was hot. Over 40 degrees he reckoned. He gradually sank down to his chin and above him Yuko said. 'Ok, you stay, I come,' and disappeared.

His mind went to the description of a bath that he read in the hotel foyer that went something like this,

"Our unique herbal steam gently exfoliates dead skin cells from all parts of your body, rejuvenating your skin while it works its wonders to relax and clear your lungs."

He knew that the human skin replaces itself every 35 days or so and he began to think that this boiling will surely speed up that process. After a few minutes he began to feel faint and he was about to climb out when he suddenly felt quite clear headed. The warmth of the water gradually penetrated his body and began to feel a strange sense of warmth and wellbeing.

Yuki left him there for nearly an hour when she came along with a huge white towel. 'Come,' she said, 'time to scrub.' She led him to a small side room that was her domain. A shelf was packed with lotions. She handed him a pair of shorts and Joe tried to examine them for they were not made of cloth. 'Paper,' said Yuko. She directed him to lay on his back then commenced an intense session of scrubbing with a rough cloth flannel, then dousing him with water. The cloth seemed too rough on his now delicate skin and certainly removed one layer.

After half an hour of this scrubbing, washing and

dousing with warm water, she took his hand and hauled him to his feet. Joe had to exclaim, 'Now I feel clean, never been as clean as this before. This bath will probably last me a week.'

Yuko looked at him strangely, 'Tomorrow you come again me bath and scrub? OK now you massage. I bring her, she said.

Her, turned out to be a Filipina named Cynthia. There was nothing typical about her because she was nearly 5' 10' heavily built, with quite a dark complexion. Joe had to ask her many questions before she admitted being from a small tribe in the Baguio hills. Conscious of secret microphones or cameras he was careful with his questions. 'You have a very nice job here. Much better than home, much more money.'

She scowled her answer whispering quite strangely, 'Everything negative.'

'I can help, maybe,' he whispered back, 'Later I will give you a phone so that you can call me.'

The massage was the Japanese method called shiatsu consisting of finger pressure and can be administered on a person fully clothed. But not here. A towel was thrown over his middle section and the massage began. After the long hot bath his muscles were soft and supple. In some areas it hurt a little but the total effect was invigorating.

Joe went to the coat hooks where his clothes were, and carefully taking out a phone and covering it with his hand, he pushed it into Cynthia's pocket, saying out loud, 'I am giving you a small gift of chocolates. It's here in your pocket. This is Cadbury chocolate, it's very good.'

After dressing, he said to Cynthia, I hope you enjoy the chocolate, but don't eat it all at once. Have some tonight before you go to sleep.'

Cynthia gave him a long hard look, the secret message

sinking in. 'I will eat it tonight before I sleep at 2 am.'

'I'll be awake then, thinking of you and the chocolate.'

He was led to the door and as he said good-bye, he said 'Don't forget to eat your chocolate.'

Next morning in his email there was a news item from the Philippines in which the government lamented the fact that "About a third of Manila's 12 million residents live in slums, and a third of 94 million Filipinos live below the poverty line of US $1.25 a day. Overall, more than half the population in Asia remains poor."

These constant reminders of the great needs of the Remy's people spurred him on to help all he could. He dialled her number, anxious for a chat. No answer. 'This line is unavailable at the moment,' said a metallic voice. That's the third day in a row, mumbled Joe.

He had only cut off the connection when there was another call from a woman who said, 'I have heard you are looking for stories about us. If you have time I will tell you mine, but I can't see you because I have to go to work. There is a place here called the Restaurant Good View. It has a second floor made of glass. We had to serve there without panties. Our skirts weren't very short but it was very embarrassing knowing people were looking up at us. On the first night I was there the girls had decided that night to wear skimpy thongs. Black ones for us Asians and white ones for the three Russian blondes. But when a regular customer complained we were made to take them off. I refused so he sent me back to my room. After a few minutes he called me to serve downstairs. The food there was very expensive because, as the menu said, the view was better!

'At the end of the shift the manager said to me, 'Why you not good girl?'

'I am good, that's why I want to wear proper clothes.'

'Good girls do what I tell them. Tonight, you are good or you go.'

'But where will I go, you mean go home to the Philippines?'

'No, you will go another place where you work every night. You live in one room and they come to see you. But very good money for you,' and grinning evilly left the room.

'The Russians girls knew about it and said, 'Better you stay here and cooperate, that place is a prostitute, no good for you. Very quick sick. Yeah, much money soon but quickly sick. What's better for you, much yarn and sick quick or much work, little money and no sick?'

'The boss kept my passport but next day I ran away to our embassy. The people there were very good and helped me get a better job at a very good restaurant, where although the work was hard, I get a good salary and they look after me very well. I was very lucky because the embassy doesn't help people find jobs. But, right at the moment I was there, the restaurant called asking if they knew anyone who needed a job.'

Then he suddenly remembered that Cynthia had not called him, or perhaps she did and he didn't hear the phone. This worried him. I wonder if they found it.

There was a vibration in his pocket, a phone call. He didn't recognize the number at first, then suddenly remembered, this would be Cynthia. 'Hullo' he said brightly. 'How are you?'

'Didn't we warn you.' It was the voice of the yakuza man he had met. 'If you do not get out of town today, then we will have to deal with you. Get out! Now! Today!' His voice rising in tone with every word. 'Out, now," he screamed. How did he know my number, goodness, he's got Cynthia's phone?

Joe immediately called Yuki and told her he was leaving for the airport. He was booked on a flight leaving late evening. He didn't want her to see him off. Doubtless they would be watching him and there was always the possibility they would antagonize her.

CHAPTER EIGHT

Not one to be easily intimidated, he decided to change his plans and cancelled the booking for Hong Kong and made one for Seoul on a plane leaving that afternoon. He texted Remy and outlined his plans, then turned off his phone so that there could be no reply or discussion. There were many thousands of Filipina workers in South Korea but he had not been asked to work there. After an overnight stay at the airport hotel, he booked on a flight to Fukuoka. He had friends there including some from the Philippines.

He was glad he was one of six foreigners when lining up at the Immigration counter in Fukuoka. There was only one man at the "Foreign Passport Counter" and one for "Japanese Passports" serving a fully loaded Jumbo Jet 747SP.

This was his second time in Fukuoka and when he came the first time a tourist officer at the airport suggested he stay with a Japanese family rather than a hotel. This was a charming young woman who, looking askance at him as they walked toward her desk said, 'In fact I wish you could stay at my house but...You will save money and meet a nice Japanese family.' He was given the address of a home about an hour's drive away and a US $100 Taxi fare. As the meter clicked over at an alarming rate he realised that this was not going to save money, only a different experience from a hotel stay. It turned out to be a restaurant and the two brothers who owned it argued as to whose home he should stay at. It was settled when he suggested he stay one night with each.

It was midnight and they insisted he have dinner, but the cook had gone home. They called her back and within a few minutes had served up a plate of noodles. He was then taken then to a small room which appeared to have no furniture but just a mat and bedcovers on the floor. This was the typical Japanese bedroom. There was no proper futon but a middle-aged servant woman fetched a few quilts some to lie on and others for a cover. She demonstrated their use by hopping into the bed she had made and coyly inviting him in. 'Out you get, there's only room for one.'

Because all the family worked at the restaurant and bar until the early hours, they slept until quite late. At 8.00 am he went looking for the bathroom in the quiet house. He tiptoed around peeking in all the doors until he found a laundry tub with a tube of toothpaste and toothbrush beside it. Believing this to be the bathroom he washed and shaved. A lady appeared and he tried to ask her where the toilet was. She didn't understand but after she had disappeared, he opened what looked like a cupboard door and there was the porcelain hole in the floor, finally he had found a toilet.

During the day he was taken to see the sights including a mountain that was completely covered with magnificent rhododendrons. The trouble was it poured heavily with rain all day and he struggled to capture the beauty on film. The cameras were soaked.

Next night was quite different. The younger brother gave him his own room in the house. It was like sleeping in a media studio. Three walls were lined with three video screens, video player, TV, a full set of hi-fi equipment, a Karaoke set with laser video, a shelf of still camera gear and a video camera. There were several shelves of videos, audio compact discs, video laser discs, records and audiocassettes.

Came the morning and he was ushered into the car and taken to the local Seven-Eleven store and asked, 'What would you like for breakfast?' The Filipino singer from the restaurant and bar who was acting as interpreter, more about her later, chose noodles, eggs and bread and then took them home to prepare the meal.

There was no question of paying for meals or accommodation. He was the very first Westerner ever to grace the restaurant and bar and their homes so he was an honoured guest. Fortunately, he happened to have some items with him that made suitable gifts.

Communication with these good Japanese people was a great problem. None of them could speak English. However, the Filipina singer, called Baby, was able to help. When he first walked into the place, they recognized each other because she had worked in his office in Manila where he was based for two years. Some of them had helped to sponsor her niece through school. Baby had become quite fluent in Japanese and had taught a few words of Filipino to her boss. Joe knew just a few words of that language and so he used these to communicate.

When he visited Fukuoka for the second time some three years later, he decided to call the friends he had made during the first visit. This was difficult because telephone area codes had changed, but eventually he got through with the help of a hotel porter who had limited English. The result was that several hours later the new Filipina waitress, Gina, called to say that her boss was coming to get him. He was an hour's drive away and he picked him up at 8.00 p.m.

He then returned to the restaurant to be greeted by the "master" of the restaurant, the elder brother and his former host. He was a little drunk but instantly recognized him and gave him the warmest and the most lengthy of welcomes. When Joe walked into the Karaoke bar, he was entertaining his customers with a song. He broke off in mid-sentence and rushed to throw his arms around me in a most un-Japanese way.

There followed loud exclamations of greetings in fractured English and Japanese and about 50 handshakes. He took him into the now closed restaurant and ordered some food. The staff complained, "The chef has gone, there is no food." His response was, "You all know how to cook some food, bring some for my guest." Soon plate of meat grilled on a bamboo stick something like satay or shiskebab appeared.

Every few minutes he would welcome Joe and shake his hand and grin from ear to ear.

The younger brother was anxious to talk to him. He had married the other Filipina he met about three years ago but their marriage was in difficulty and she had gone home to Manila. For an hour he acted as marriage counsellor and promised to write to her and encourage her to go back to her husband as she had returned to the Philippines.

His interpreter, the Filipina waitress, then disclosed that she was married to a Japanese man and that they were now separated and could he help them. By this time his host was completely drunk and younger brother decided it was time to take him back to the hotel. They talked of his marriage problems all the way and then for an hour in the hotel room. Whenever there was a lull in the conversation, the interpreter slipped in a question or two about her own problem. Gina also had a friend who needed help and asked him to see her.

Joe felt sad for these two couples whose main problems were directly related to the vast cultural differences between Japan and the Philippines.

The hotel in Fukuoka wasn't exactly top class but the manners of the staff were. A waitress would stop one meter short of the table, give a slight bow, and then place the item on the table. And this was only the coffee shop where a humble breakfast of scrambled eggs, toast and coffee cost US $17.00, at home it would be about five.

Joe wondered how they would serve a meal in the modest restaurant on the top floor where the cheapest three-course dinner cost US $75.00 and the most expensive $300 per person. Come to think of it, probably the same.

Japan is such a neat orderly place, and oh so clean. Taxis are immaculate often with white-gloved drivers and white seat covers. But so is everything else clean: even a cement mixer shines like a well-kept Rolls Royce.

Next night Joe called to see Gina's friend who worked in another bar. It was hemmed in between two garishly lit nightclubs. After a drink or two he asked to see her after work. She called the mamasan who explained that if he wanted to see her, he had to pay $100. 'But she is a friend of my friend, we only want to talk,' protested Joe.

The Mamasan was having nothing of it. 'Gina work here for me, you want her you pay. You stay here $100, you go someplace else pay $200, come back 8 o'clock. Give me credit card ok.' He hadn't thought about needing an expense account of that sort.

Elena's English was quite good and so he asked her if it was better to go out or stay there. 'Let's go out.'

A look of alarm spreading across her face. 'I can't talk here, so they took a taxi back to his hot. The hotel reception staff took no notice of him leading a girl to the lift and the security man based on his floor merely lifted a thumb as if to say, 'That's OK.'

As Joe turned back from locking the door Elena flung herself at him, weeping. 'Can you take me away from here?' She began to cry loudly saying something that Joe could not understand.

'Let's sit down and talk about it,' as he led her towards the only armchair in the room. He pushed her down, but she immediately sprang up and clung to him. He moved to the bed and sat down with Elena sitting close by pressing up against him. 'Now no more tears, just settle down and tell me what is wrong.'

Between sobs that slowly subsided, she told her story. Answering an advertisement in a Manila paper she was informed that there was a very good job in southern Japan. She would be the maître 'd in a good restaurant. She would earn in a month as much as she would earn in a year at home. There would be free food and accommodation.

'Some things were true; I have a very small room just big enough for one tatami mat. No cupboards or a wardrobe, just plastic bags that I hang on nails on the wall. The rice is ok but not enough with vegetables and meat. No fish. No time for friends. No day off. No phone calls home. No getting a call from home. She took my cell phone. And no money.'

'What do you mean no money?'

'The Mamasan has got my ticket and passport and she says I have to pay all the expenses of coming here first. Pay for visa, ticket, room, food, everything. When contract finish, she pays. That more eighteen months.'

They talked for an hour. A story of broken promises. There was a family at home who were expecting some money every month to help pay for their many expenses. After six months she had sent nothing home. 'What will they be thinking of me? All my promises broken. Their letters make me very sad.'

But there was something else Joe wanted to know. 'Why did the Mamasan want $200 from me? What's that for?'

Elena looked at him, incredulously. 'You don't know? You don't know? She's selling me. She's selling this,' patting her abdomen, 'It's yours for $200.'

'No, no, I can't do that.'

'You paid for it.'

'Oh Elena, I am so sorry for you. I promise I am going to help you.'

As best he could, without giving away too much information, Joe tried to explain why he was in Japan. He soon had a dozen names of people Elena knew who worked near her place. She believed that half of them were not being treated well. Some were just plain prostitutes.

It was now 2 am and Joe said that it was time for him to take her back. 'You can't do that now, it's too late. They will be closed. I go back at 8 o'clock. I stay here with you.'

Joe had twin beds so he showed her where to sleep. He changed into his pyjamas in the bathroom and got into bed. Elena then went to the bathroom and came back in her undies and hopped into the other bed.

An hour later he was almost asleep when he felt Elena getting into his bed. 'I can't sleep,' she whispered, 'not with you right here. I am not selling myself, but I want you. I think I love you.' She took his face in her hands and began to kiss him. Long sweet kisses. Her hand moved down his back, then up again.

Joe soon realized what she wanted, needed. She needed someone to love her, to show her true affection. She doesn't need sex, she needs love.

'Oh Elena, I am so sorry you have had such a bad experience. But this is not right. You must get back into your own bed. Go. You can't stay here. We'll talk some more in the morning.'

There is a multi-million-dollar hostessing business in Japan. Deals are done, alliances formed and mergers forged in dimly lit hostess bars. There are hostess bars in every community employing huge numbers of women. They form a relaxed environment from confining offices, someone has called them 'an oasis of scotch and water and pretty women.' Business deals can be carried out in a relaxed environment. But for the most part, the women involved are pretty foreigners, preferably blonds, or Japanese women of class and character.

With some notable exceptions the Filipinas are sometimes confined to the seedier side of the business. Not all of the hostess bars offer sexual services. After being served multiple drinks there are many occasions when the client begins to talk sex. The hostesses will either provide what he wants or calls on a pretty back-room girl, and often as not, she will be a foreigner. There are numbers of South Americans, Europeans as well as girls from various Southeast Asian countries. It is in this industry that some Filipinas have been trapped.

Leny called a friend, Odette, whom she knew was in a difficult position. A competent singer and dancer, her 'entertainers' job did not turn out to be one in which she could exercise her lovely singing voice, but it was her body that her employer wanted to sell. She was housed in a commodious room upstairs from the hostess bar, and was on call for twelve hours a day, or should we say night. Expected to be on duty from 6 pm, she would first report to a makeup artist brought in every day to prepare her for customers who would be considered important businessmen. The blond downstairs had plied the man with drink and after his business was completed, she would bring him upstairs to be entertained by Odette. 'I have to offer him anything from a cuddle, a massage, sex or anything he wants,' she said. 'Mostly the men are quite nice to me, and not all of them want sex,' she says, 'and they usually give me good tips, but it's not want I want to do.'

Odette spent all her time in her room, which was designed as a studio with a bed and a kitchenette well stocked with food and drink provided by her employer. It was equipped with television, music DVDs, a radio, and a large range of pornographic DVDs. Sometimes her client wants only to watch pornography. But she found the work debasing and after nine months was quite depressed and demoralized. There is a computer but it is not connected to the Internet. The only phone permitted is programmed for local calls. Her six-month work visa had expired and her employer refuses to give her passport back so that she could apply for an extension. 'They think I will run away home: and I will too if I get the chance.' Odette is allowed out for personal shopping once a week and is always chaperoned by her employer.

Lynette was 19 when she first went to Japan. 'They had offered me a good job as an entertainer that I took to mean a singer and dancer. My boss had several bars and nightclubs, and he would send me to a different one every month. The work was hard in that I used to start at 6.30 pm for practice and finish at about 3 am with two days off every month. We lived upstairs on the 3rd floor of the main club.

'I was part of a small group of 2 boys and 3 girls, and we would sing in English, Tagalog and Japanese. It was a very good experience for me and I sent lots of money home.

'There was a bad side though. My boss was always overcharging people especially when they were drunk. I complained about that and he was angry with me.

'But he told us to let him know if any of the customers gave us trouble and he would storm over to their table and yell at them and threaten to report them to the police. Strangely, this happened several times, yet those same men came back again and again.

'At his other club there was problem with the system the manager there allowed the girls go to with customer outside. They found the Japanese men very good and were always willing to help the Filipina. Some just gave money others wanted sex too. Maybe 50% had sex with them.'

'Really, that much? Is that true? It's not fair to say that about everyone.'

'I suppose I don't really know but you just have that feeling from what everyone says. But it's always a secret deal, the manager becomes not involved.

'I've got a good husband and with my money now I have a *sarisari* store. I also lend money at 10% but my husband doesn't know that.'

CHAPTER NINE

After three days Joe took a flight to Manila as arranged by the embassy. Seated next to him was a journalist from Manila who was full of questions as to what Joe was planning to do in his city. 'I know everything you need to know about Manila,' he boasted, 'and I can show you everything and anything, all the tourist spots, the restaurants and all the places where you can have a good time.' He was full of questions about Joe's plans and Joe had to try and assure him that he was just a simple tourist - a former resident even, coming back to see the place where he and his family lived many years ago.

His newfound friend, Ricardo, actually kept from Joe the fact that he was a journalist. He was simply looking for a story and sensed that Joe might be a person of interest. They talked about the Filipinas that lived abroad and the important contribution they made to families and economies around the world. But when he discovered that Joe knew Remy he became very excited. 'Not Remy whose mother used to work at the palace? And she's with the government or something?'

'Do you know her?'

'Know her! She's my wife's cousin.'

'I hope she will meet me at the airport.'

'What's going on then, between you two?'

It took a while for Joe to explain how they met but didn't go into any details about the work he had got into.

'Do you mind if we do a story about you. How you used to live and work here in the days of President Marcos and now have come back for a visit of nostalgia? I'll assign one of my staff to do it. I'm what we call the staff coordinator at a local newspaper. We specialize in human-interest stories. But I'll have to talk to Remy because she is more than a maid. How on earth did you get her to be your maid?'

Remy's greeting at the airport was warm and at the same time very puzzled as to how Joe and Ricardo had met. As soon as she could, she tried to caution Joe about talking too much. 'We don't want publicity, it's best if we work quietly. Not everyone likes what we do.' That puzzled Joe no end. But next morning there was a quiet knock on his hotel room door and there stood an attractive young woman, notebook in hand. She smiled brightly and said, 'Ricardo sent me, you have a story for us?' and proffered a name card, Baby Mirador, *Manila Daily Times - Your Paper*.

'You had better come In. Yes we can talk but not about a story.' This was the beginning of a long conversation when Joe tried to explain that they did not wish for any publicity at the moment. He was in the process of promising to release the story to her at the appropriate time when there was another knock on the door. This time it was Remy. In the sweetest way possible she soon had Baby on her way adding to the promise of a story later. Half an hour later Ricardo appeared and this resulted in him promising to run a story of a former resident returning to see Manila after an absence of many years. All very simple and non-controversial he assured them.

Late that evening Baby called him on his newly purchased local cell phone. 'How did you get my number?'

'Ricardo gave it to me. But I would like to see you again, not for work, just to see you. Would you like that?' Mmm, she's a bit forward thought Joe. But she's nice though, maybe they could meet for dinner he suggested.

'Good, I'll come to you and you can call room service.'

'You are a bit cheeky aren't you? OK come when you are ready.'

'I'm ready now,' and with that there was a tap on his door, and there stood Baby, grinning from ear to ear, cell phone in hand.

They talked and talked late into the night in between mouthfuls of lechon, the famous Philippine roast pork. The result was that this young woman was obviously looking for a foreign partner, preferably an American but a New Zealander would do. 'I am sure we could make a go of it,' admitted Joe, 'but I am twenty years older than you.'

'But I would only want one child,' said Baby and sold herself as a good caring wife and mother in the way many of her people can be so frank. Tears were not far from her eyes when she left at 11 pm, and Joe's heart went out to her. Giving her a warm hug, all he could say was, 'I'm sorry, but there might be someone else.' The Philippines is one of the few countries of the world where families are often very happy for one of their number to marry a foreigner. This has resulted in many very happy mixed marriages.

He lay on the bed and thought about what he had said - there might be someone else. Deep down he realized, he had been thinking about Remy. If it is going to be anyone, I think it has to be Remy. The more he thought about this, the more he began to understand that maybe he was falling in love with her. He decided that in the meantime, he would say nothing. But every time he thought of Remy in this way, he also thought of Renny.

Thoughts of that nature were far from Remy's mind next morning when she appeared with a newspaper thrusting it at him saying, 'Didn't we agree no newspaper interviews?' At the top of the third page stood the headline in thick bold letters 'NEW ZEALANDER HERE TO HELP HAPLESS FILIPINAS.' It was cleverly done. A few snatches of comment, much speculation and imaginative writing had Joe portrayed as the saviour of many women in trouble around the world. In general, the tenor of the article was true if not factual. 'I am going to see my people now and explain what happened, let's hope they will understand. Meantime you had better change hotels. Go to this one in Quezon City, it's out of the way and well clear of this area. Don't talk to anyone, especially the taxi driver. Tell him you are Australian and you've come to meet the child you sponsor. The Compassion International office is near there so the story will look good.'

'Actually, I do sponsor children through them and have done so for twenty-five years so I'll and see them today.'

The Compassion director was very gracious despite the burdens she carried. 'Look at this,' she said, hold ing up many sheets of computer printouts listing thousands of children currently being sponsored. 'This too.' It was another long list of names of children waiting for sponsors. 'The economic situation here is still very bad and there are so many poor families desperate for help to educate their children.'

Joe had a key question, 'How many of these children have mothers and fathers overseas who are supporting their families?'

'None,' was the quick answer. 'If they have a parent overseas then their basic needs will be met. It's the ones who don't have any support that we register for sponsors.

'I have some visitors whom you may like to meet. Their pastor sent them to us because they have just suffered a terrible tragedy. The lady's sister was able to get a job in Denmark but two days after arriving there she was killed in a bus accident at a railroad level crossing. She was killed instantly. It was a terrible accident because the bus wasn't hit by the train, the bus hit the train. The driver must have gone to sleep or had a heart attack or something and drove right into the side of it. The children had been so happy and were sure that aunty would help them every month. It cost the extended family a lot of money for her to get the job now they are poverty stricken and deep in debt. We can't help with the debt but we can get the kids educated and that's insurance for the future.'

Just after breakfast next morning Remy called Joe to say that her appointment with her people had been cancelled because they had to be out of town that day. She suggested that he go back to the Compassion office and ask to be taken to families with whom they are in touch. He knew that that would not be as straightforward as she suggested because it takes a few days to arrange such meetings. To begin with, it is necessary to have a police good behaviour certificate from their own country. One child sponsorship agency had terrible trouble when they discovered that several paedophiles had been visiting their sponsored children and had interfered with them. The story appeared in TIME magazine much to the dismay of the agency. But there was something Joe had never disclosed to Remy, it was that at one time he was the Asia director of Compassion International, and maybe he thought, they would cooperate with him.

This was pre-computer days and the staff searched the files until they came to Joe's era some twenty years earlier. The senior staff agreed with their director that Joe was not a risk to the children and that they could bend the rules.

He was taken to an area not far from the international airport where there were many hundreds of families living beside old canals and waterways. Their rough unpainted wooden houses were jammed together along the banks. 'These are not the poorest of the poor,' said his guide, 'but they are too poor to have better housing. The poorest have even simpler dwellings, usually just a few pieces of old plywood and plastic sheeting and some can be found on the huge refuse dumps about the city. We are not going there because they have had too much publicity. As soon as an Americano (i.e. any white foreigner) appears, they will flock around him expecting handouts. Even trying to interview someone will cost money. They will want a thousand Pesos even to talk to you. Foreign press has spoiled them.'

They walked along a narrow path between ungainly lines of houses and children skipped and danced around them. They weren't shy to ask for money. 'Peso,' they called, until the Compassion guide told them to behave and go away. An old man with snow white hair and clad only in a dirty pair of shorts shouted for them to be quiet and go away. Joe's guide, Fredrick, sniggered and said, 'Guess what he said? He said, 'go away, don't be like the rats who come out at night to sniff at everything."

They returned to the main road another way passing down another dirty lane of ramshackle houses. Fredrick explained that this was an area where they did not sponsor children. The main reason was that it was such a mobile population. As soon as someone earns enough money to rent a better place they are out of here and it is difficult to keep track of them. This visit, therefore, was easy for Fred because the people here did not know about their sponsorship programme. Otherwise they would be all over him. 'Besides,' he said. There are no churches and we only work with and through churches because they know the people and the ones who need and deserve help.'

Later over a coffee, Joe asked Fred, 'what hope have any of the people I saw today of getting out of the poverty cycle?'

The answer was fast coming. 'If an adult can get good job, and that's very difficult, or if one of the family gets a job overseas, and that's also very difficult because they can't raise the money for an application.'

'There is someone you should meet,' said Remy next morning. 'We already know all about her and her story is recorded but it would be good if you could talk with her. She needs to hear that we are trying to do something for our people overseas. She had a terrible experience that has left her severely depressed, for her sake it would be good for her to tell you about it. She will be here soon.'

Joe recorded her story as follows as she recounted her experience in Doha.

Lena could smell smoke. She looked out the window and it was coming up from below to reach her on the fifth floor. There was a little coming through under the door. She ran across the room and tried to open it. It was locked. But that was normal. She had been locked in the apartment for five months. Her employers usually left the apartment after breakfast and returned at any time during the evening. Lena was nanny to five-month-old girl seven days a week. The mother would not spend more than an hour with the child every day. She left all the bathing, feeding and dressing to Lena.

Lena was taken to a huge supermarket on Sunday afternoons when she decided on the food needed for the week. Her employer made no decisions in regard to food because Lena was not just nanny and housemaid but cook as well. Every morning she prepared breakfast and then the evening meal. But to her utter frustration she would never know if the family would eat at home after work. At least half of the time they would come in late and curtly say, 'We've eaten, throw it out.'

The day for Lena began at about five a.m. or whenever the child woke up. The baby, Fatima, slept in a bassinette beside Lena's bed and had done so since she was two months old and she had become a precious loving child.

Lena lent out the window such as it was. It was hardly big enough for her head, as it was not intended for ventilation in this fully air-conditioned building. The air conditioning had not been working that day and the room had become stifling hot. The baby lay in her bed naked and Lena herself wore only a cotton housecoat with no underwear.

Shouting for help at the top of her voice, she could see people gathering down below calling to her to come down. 'The door is locked, I have no key, I'm number 8,' she yelled back. The smoke began to billow up the side of the building choking her. The room was filling with smoke. She grabbed the baby and held her close and lay on the floor gasping for air. Desperate to protect the child she opened her housecoat and tucked the baby inside and buttoned it up again, holding the baby close. Fatima began to cry then sensing where she was, her tiny mouth found a nipple and began to suck. This sent shockwaves through the woman and immediately began to remember her own baby who was back at home in the care of her sister. Would she ever see her again? Her mind was in turmoil. The building was on fire, the room was filling with smoke, the door was locked, the baby was desperately seeking comfort, she thought about the two maids who died in a fire in Doha only a month ago, and the baby was beginning to be affected by the smoke. Insanely she thought about the way she had intended to cut the child's fingernails that morning as she could feel her scratching and clawing at her chest.

Holding the child close she got up and found a towel and tried to soak it in the wash hand basin she had in her *en suite*. But the water was off. She tried the shower. Nothing. By this time the smoke was becoming very thick so she crawled back to the bedroom and lay on the floor near the window. She began to pray, crying out 'Lord help me, help us. Forgive me my sin. The baby is ok she's got no sin. I've got sin Lord. Save me. Send the firemen. I didn't come here to die. Save me Lord.'

When firemen broke down her door, they found her unconscious. A fireman grabbed Lena and threw her over his shoulder in the typical fireman's grip, but in the turmoil, he did not realize that there was a tiny baby under her housecoat. He jogged down the stairs Lena bouncing on his shoulder but her body was crushing the unconscious baby. By the time he had unloaded them in the ambulance the child was crushed to death. As he leant over and dropped Lena on her back onto the stretcher the nurse noticed something strange about the body and soon found the baby. An ambulance took them to the hospital where the child was declared dead on arrival. Lena recovered after a few days and was sent back to the Philippines. But not before she tried to find out about the baby. A kindly nurse told her that she had not survived the fire and gave details of her tragic death.

'Tonight, we go to my place for dinner. My mother is home again after her trip to the U.S., and you know she is a great cook and she'll spoil you.' But her greeting that evening startled Joe. Enclosing him a warm embrace and kissing both cheeks. Hmm, she kissed me on both cheeks when I notice the people here usually kiss on one cheek. Joe's heart had been quickened by the contact with beautiful women of late, and as he observed the way Renny served the meal and chatted so warmly, he began to think of the time they shared together and that she was a candidate for the now awakened desire for a wife. She's just the right age, size, and demeanour – everything is right about her! Perish the thought; it's not a year since my wife died.

Next morning there was another meeting with the officials when they discussed the situation in many countries. 'Take Saudi Arabia for instance,' said Rico, 'I think it was about 2010 when they brought in over 200,000 workers from the Philippines that was in only one year. You remember when the Americans decided to have a special push in Afghanistan; they called it a 'final surge' or something like that. They sent in a large number of extra troops. They required over 2,000 more workers to service this and a great number of these were from the Philippines.

'There are employment organizations all over the country and they do important work but always there are people out to make money the easy way. They make promises of good well-paying jobs and take fees from the people who have to borrow money only to have been deceived and they end up in worse debt. Some of them make fake documents even passports.

'You don't have to worry about this as we have local police and other organizations trying to uncover these scams, we want you to concentrate on places overseas where our people have trouble.

'Generally speaking, the people of the Middle East do not respect Asians. Many of them are workers no more no less. As such, they have no rights; their position in life is to serve their masters without question. If they are Christians then their position is sometimes even worse because they are unbelievers, kaffirs, the lowest of the low. As far as fundamental Muslim believers are concerned, they hardly deserve to live while they are in rejection of Muhammad. Some take the Koran at its word where it states several times that if a person will not accept Mohammad, he doesn't deserve to live.

'Then the status of women is difficult. Some take literally the statement in the Koran that says 'Man is superior to women' in Sura 4. 'Men are superior to woman on account of the qualities with which God has gifted the one above the other.'

A local paper had an article about this continuing problem stating that it was difficult to describe the working conditions of many household service workers except as virtual slaves. Slavery was abolished by royal decree in 1962, but customs are apparently hard to overcome. Domestic workers continue to be treated as slaves in some royal and aristocratic households, and this behaviour is reproduced by those lower in the social hierarchy.

AN EMPLOYMENT AGENCY

'I would like to visit one of the employment agencies and observe how they operate. My former secretary Louie lives here now and I know one of her best friends owns an agency. I will contact her and see what she can arrange.'

'Yes, that's a good idea, go ahead and see what you can find out,' said Remy, her boss nodding his head in agreement.

Within ten minutes of calling Louie, she was back on the phone with an appointment already set up. There seemed to a great number of these companies, perhaps hundreds, specialising in overseas contract workers.

The owner and managing director warmly welcomed Joe and called in her assistant. 'I will hand you over to Annalisa and she will arrange for you to interview applicants. Most of them have already served one term overseas and are applying for new contracts.' Over the next three days, small groups of young women were brought to Joe where he interviewed them in his hotel room. Every one of the twenty-nine that he spoke to had a different story.

The first one was Rose, aged 31, a single mother of one child whom she left with her mother. Working for a Kuwaiti family, Rose never had a day off for seven months, 'not even an hour,' she said. 'But my biggest problem was that I was not allowed a cell phone nor could I use my employer's phone to contact home. For all that time I had no communication at all with my family. My madam was very strict and gave me charge of her twin daughters aged 7 months. But I could never do anything right or please her in any way. She hardly ever touched the children herself maybe holding one or the other, but never both at the same time, and only for a couple of minutes every few days. She left me to do everything.'

'The problem she had was that she was unable to have any more children and her husband was furious that she could not bear him a son.'

'I was able to change my job but the next one wasn't much better. Sixteen hours a day, every day, looking after a family of 6 adults. I had to do all the cleaning and cooking. The cooking was difficult because each of the six was on a different diet. That meant usually six different meals twice a day. One had a seafood allergy, there was a vegetarian, a vegan, one was fish only no meat, another had a problem with milk but the father ate everything. I always made pasta and noodles for every meal and doctored some of it up to suit them all.'

'But' said Rose, 'I learned a lot about cooking and stayed with them for 18 months. My salary was always very late but by the end of the contract they had paid me in full. Next time I will try for a job in Dubai. I value the cooking skills I developed while I was with them.'

Albertina, a single woman of 34, spent four years in Singapore. Her responsibility was to teach English to the three children of the family. Her only problem was with the grandmother who felt that Albertina ate too much. 'In fact, it got so embarrassing I used to eat alone in the toilet. Can you imagine that? In my family we always ate together at least once a day. Eating together was always a symbol of love for each other and that we were happy to be a family. But here I often eat alone in the toilet! The problem was that this Chinese family did not eat rice and refused to buy it for me. They were from north China where the main staple is wheat and therefore could not understand why I needed rice.'

'A Jordanian police general and Palestinian wife employed me for nearly three months,' said Venline, a 29-year-old single woman. 'I came to love these people and their 5 children. They treated me as one of the family, and we could laugh and joke together. They paid me properly and gave me a day off every month but I was so lonely without my own family. In a strange sort of way, the more I enjoyed their family the more I missed my own. I would stand in front of the mirror and think how alone I was. My only consolation was that every month I could send most of my salary home and then hear how my younger siblings were all doing well at school, because I was paying all their fees.'

Lynrose was still smarting after five months in Amman, the capital and largest city of Jordan. It is the country's political, cultural and commercial centre and one of the oldest continuously inhabited cities in the world. She worked as a domestic helper for a Palestinian couple who treated her and the two other helpers with respect. 'But we had to tie up our hair and hide it all the time.' In fact, they did their best to persuade Lynrose to convert from being a Roman Catholic Christian to a Muslim. If she did that they promised to take her to Mecca. She refused.

Five months without a single day off and a constant battle with the madam who did not speak a word of English, and no communication with home, made this five-foot Filipina plan to run away. There were three children in the home and the house staff were not permitted to speak any English to them. 'The only Arabic words I know are the bad words: it's important to learn the bad words first,' grinned Lynrose.

'I hated to see the way my family struggled, that's why I got the job. I started work at 13 and I am determined to see that my two younger sisters get a good education.'

Lauda was one of 37 servants employed by a high-ranking Dubai prince. They came from Sri Lanka, India and the Philippines. Lauda was a personal servant of the princess, but they did not get on. They lived in a large palace in Dubai but Lauda had to keep to the princess's part of the building and must never be seen anywhere else. One day, when the air conditioning was turned down, the princess caught her wiping her brow. 'How dare you do that in front of me,' and slapped her face twice.

'I guess she was a very unhappy woman as she was separated from the prince, and I don't know if there were other wives. I suppose having borne three daughters was the real problem.'

Lauda confesses that she never ate better in her life as the food was abundant with lots of tropical fruit always available. But she didn't like me and I didn't like her so they gave me a ticket home after just a month.

'I am 31,' began Nora, 'and I am single although I have had three husbands. My first two died and I divorced the third. I am going abroad so that I can help my 29-year-old sister who is pregnant. She's single and lives in a poor-quality nipa hut that is very close to the shore. When the spring tide is high, it comes into the house so we need to move to higher ground. So twice a day the water swishes across the floor bringing with it garbage so it's a big job to clean it out every time.

The job I have in Dubai is just what I need to help my little family.

Teresita brought her whole family to meet Joe. The five of them sat on his bed and her angelic five-year-old daughter, looked around and said, 'why can't we all sleep here? It's a big bedroom for us all!' While working in Dubai, Teresita fell in love with a very tall black American sailor. They had a child but unfortunately, he was transferred to another port and they have lost contact. But he was very generous to her family. 'Even though he was so tall and big, he was so gentle with me and I used to laugh about his large feet. It was always difficult for him to buy shoes and he looked after them his as though they were his babies.'

This young woman was one of the many Filipinas working on cruise ships around the world. She worked as a stewardess for three years for a Norwegian company then in a hotel restaurant in Dubai. 'But it was better on the ship,' she says,' because I find that many of the Arabs are sexual maniacs. They are always touching us. When placing a plate or glass on the table they will feel our fingers or arms or touch our legs and bottoms. They are always asking us for phone numbers and sometimes they come straight out with it and ask for sex, right there at the table, like they will give their card with the room number saying, 'Come see me later.' I can say that this happened to me at least once every day. There were a number of Chinese and Russian prostitutes based in the hotel but many men like to get Filipinas if they can. We are clean and, I'm sorry to say, some of our women don't charge as much. Some of the married women are so greatly tempted when they are offered as much as a month's salary for just an hour or so with someone.'

'Whenever a problem arose our manager, an Indian man, would never side with us. He refused to listen to our complain about the customers.'

There were several young women who had been duped by illegal and unlicenced employment companies. Jenny, whose marriage was annulled at 42, and mother of three, paid an agency US$800.00 for a job in Romania. She had her own passport (they offered to get an illegal one) and paid off the government agencies that are supposed to monitor overseas workers' contracts. A relative owned the company and he organised everything for her so that she did not have to attend any compulsory training courses.

They took an enormous risk in doing this because if they were found out the penalty is severe. 'Look at this,' holding out a sheet of paper, 'this is a quotation from a law book, - it says a) Any person found guilty of illegal recruitment shall suffer the penalty of imprisonment of not less than six (6) years and one (1) day but not more than twelve (12) years and a fine not less than two hundred thousand pesos (P200,000.00) nor more than five hundred thousand pesos (P500,000.00).'

Her first job was as a domestic helper to a rich family, or as she put it, 'A rich corrupt government family.' But she only lasted a month before being moved to an international hotel chain of good repute. Problem was the agency that supplied the housekeeping staff did not abide by the rules and required Jenny to work 10 hours a day, 7 days a week.

After a few months she was moved to a large house to become one of the 8 servants plus 6 security men. This family had two beautifully furnished and decorated homes in the countryside plus another in the city. Her employer liked Jenny and often gave her presents and quite large sums of money (E 500) to spend on her day off. But this was to encourage me to share myself with him. This created jealousy among her colleagues because the others received only half that amount.

'My life is not a good example to others. I was married at 18 after a five-year friendship with a boyfriend. I was still in college when I became pregnant. Just before the wedding I had an abortion but this failed. My husband turned out to be a drunkard and a gambler and got into drugs', Jenny added.

'I'm too old to get an overseas job now so I have a small *sari-sari* store', Jenny concluded.

Getting a job with the American military in Iraq sounded too good to be true for 46-year-old Lisa. She was lucky to get a job at her age. The military gave a private company the contract to handle the maintenance of the camp. The employment agency was certain that, because they would be working for the Americans, it would be a well-paid job with plenty of special privileges. But the only privilege she got was a 12-hour day seven days a week as a 'housekeeping foreman.' In other words, she was in charge of cleaning a huge ablution block. There were about 10,000 Filipinas on the base when she first arrived. The men and women were lodged in separate camps with a 10 pm curfew, as she put it, 'to prevent pregnancies.' Lisa worked continuously for two years, including Christmas Day and New Year's Day and saved nearly all her salary. 'That was easy,' she said, 'there was nothing to buy in the desert and now I have paid for my three children through university.'

'She never dared hit me like she was always hitting the others.' This was Grace a strong looking 46-year-old. Not a typical slightly built Filipina but a sturdy 70 kg. 'The madam in my house was always hitting the other two servants from Indonesia and Sri Lanka, but not me.'

After spending three years in Taiwan taking care of a 75-year-old woman (a work I love) Grace took a job in Dubai. This was with a family of three children, the mother from Kuwait and father from the Emirates. Grace was nanny to the youngest, a boy of 8 and helped an Indian man with the cooking and slept with the boy at night.

'My main problem was with the mother: she was always shouting at me. I thought she was a little crazy but perhaps deep down she sensed that her husband liked me too much. Whenever we were alone, he would touch me and invite me to secretly go out with him. He often tried to give me presents of money and jewellery but I always refused to accept them and tried to avoid him all the time. Then when my contract was finished, he asked me to marry him. What an impossible thing that would be for me! He was allowed more than one wife and there was no way it would work. First of all, I would have to convert to Islam, then deny my Philippine citizenship, and how could I live with that other wife? He's already got two boys so he'd be marrying me for sex. But I am not small and dainty. Before I went there someone told me to be careful because some Arab men like big fat women and I'm certainly fatter than his wife.

'The wife did her best to torment me. Often, she would scold then hit the other servants. One was a small Indonesian woman who was easily intimidated and the Indian cook had no backbone. One day she found some vegetables we had not used and had become stale. She attempted to force an old carrot into my mouth screaming "You eat this." I shoved her away with my elbow squashing her breast and she cried out in pain. Then she turned to the cook and slapped him across the face. But she never dared touch me again.

'My boss was an immigration police official and was often out of town and that was when she was the most difficult. Sometimes she refused to give us food when he was away so I would go out and buy some for the three of us.'

'One day when she was having her regular sulk, I suggested to the others to go to their embassies to complain. But they simply said that they would not even be heard if they complained, declaring that they were not concerned about them. I have to say that the Philippine government is very good in attempting to protect their people overseas."

'I fell in love with an Indian-Arab mix man in Dubai man and converted to Islam. But now I don't know what to do as life is so complicated. I have three children at home, never married properly, in love with this man, he's in Dubai and doesn't have a passport, I'm here, getting older all the time, needing money, what to do?'

Mary, single, aged 25, was leaving the country tomorrow, and very excited about her new contract. She was to care for a newborn baby in Dubai. After three years in Dubai with a family of three small children whose parents who had no idea how to raise children, she was determined to teach and train this new baby the right way to live.

'My Arab family had no idea how to handle the children like when to eat or sleep. The mother was 35 and was always covered up with just her eyes showing even in the house and that was quite unusual. Mostly, the Muslim women in Dubai wore regular clothing in the house and covered up only when they went outdoors. She was studying at the university and most of the time I just ignored her. She never spoke to me except to complain and certainly I would never speak to her: we never even exchanged greetings. You can imagine how uncomfortable it was for me living like that because here we greet everybody all the time. Fortunately, there were five of us helping in their house, a nanny for each child, a cook and a laundress.

'All the nannies were mothers themselves so they were good with the kids but we could never discipline them in front of the parents, not even a little bit. When the four-year-old boy would beat us with his fists the parents would just smile and gave the impression that they thought he was very clever knowing how to treat the servants.

'I did my best to finish the contract and although they never paid me according to the agreement while I was there, I hoped they would by time I left. All of my salary was sent by them directly to the Philippines and thankfully, by the end of two years, there was enough to buy a small coconut plantation for the family.

'Not being able to communicate regularly with home was very difficult for me. I was not allowed to have a cell phone but they gave the cook one to use for ordering food supplies. Sometimes he would lend it to me and I would hide in the toilet when I called home.

'At the end of two years continuous work, never a day off, not even an hour, I was very tired. Very often it was 2 am before I got to bed and always up at 5.30.'

Elizabeth, 28, a single mother with 4-year-old son, spent a year in Qatar, one of three Filipina domestic helpers taking care of two huge houses. 'My family was still living in the past when rich people had slaves. That's what we were. We had to be up at 4 am and did not get to sleep until 11 pm. No days off. During the Ramadan fasting month it was even worse. We got about 2 hours sleep a night. I collapsed with fatigue and spent two nights in hospital. Then my boss came and took me home shouting at me all the way saying that I was a lazy good-for-nothing bitch. For a Muslim to call a woman a female dog was a very great insult.

'I was down to 40 kg. and when I contacted my agent but they told me to go back to work and stop complaining telling me it was not unusual to work every day.

'My two colleagues were also from my country but they were Muslims and despised me because I was a Four-Square Gospel Christian. They used to gloat about not having to work as hard as me. They got the easy jobs like to chaperone the girls of the family who were 22 and 26 years old and were never allowed to be alone outside the house. They didn't do any work inside or outside the house. They sat around waiting for someone to marry them. I don't think they knew how to make a cup of tea. The older one was getting worried because it was time she was married and this made her very angry and moody. She would spit and snarl at me such as if I was in the way when she wanted to walk past, she would yell, 'Get out of my way."

Sally ran away twice from her employers in Dubai. Her

Emirate family treated her so badly she couldn't stand it any longer so she ran away and reported them to the agency. They told her to pay them the Ps60,000 she owed them or go back to work. She tried again but after a few weeks ran away a second time. She met an Indian lady in the mall who found her another job where she worked for two years. But in fact, she was living illegally there along with thousands of others in a similar situation. Then the Sheik declared an amnesty for runaways and so she was able to go back to the Philippines.

Returning to the Middle East she found a job with a family in Qatar. The husband was Syrian and wife Lebanese and they treated her kindly. Not being allowed to go to church, they advised her to dress like a Muslim but pray to Jesus. She even kept the fast but on returning home became a Roman Catholic again.

But being back at home had its problems. Her husband was an illegal gold miner but she was not happy living with him describing him as 'sexually unkind.' Leaving her 12-month-old baby with her parents-in-law, Sally is returning to her family in Qatar.

CHAPTER TEN

The manager of the recruitment agency said, 'These young women are not all angels; sometimes they get into all sorts of trouble for doing illegal things.' Louie was a good example. She got a job as a domestic helper in Hong Kong.

But her employer, a military doctor, was quite strange. He and his wife had no understanding of bringing up children. They had a boy with a harelip and allowed him free rein, and never disciplined him whatsoever. When the parents weren't looking, he would kick her. But Louie was very strict with him and when they were alone, she would smack him if necessary. When his parents went out, he would say to Louie 'I'm a good boy.' One time the parents asked, 'Why does he say that every time we go out?' And Louie thought, that's because he knows I'll give him a hiding if he is naughty!

She was not allowed to use a mop to clean the floor but had to get down on her hands and knees and use a cloth. Cleaning the toilet was very strange: they insisted she should not use a cloth but only her hands. She soon got sick of that and broke her contract and took a job in an office. She was positioned near the door so that she could spot immigration inspectors doing their rounds. Her employers were pleased with her so sent her to university to learn Cantonese, and then made her the receptionist.

When the immigration inspectors came, she hid out the back and could watch through a one-way mirror. But after a year, it was decided that it was too dangerous to continue like this so she got a job as a domestic helper in the home of a Chinese couple. On completing her two-year contract with them, a stewardess of China Airlines employed her and they became good friends and when she was married in Taiwan, invited Louie to attend the wedding.

On her weekly day off she would go to the place on Victoria Island where many Filipinas like to congregate. She often would meet girls who were not happy with the accommodation provided by their employers so she found an inexpensive flat for rent and then sublet it to a few domestic helpers. A friendly Chinese businessman helped her (illegally) by signing all the documents. This worked out well so she acquired another flat and had a nice little business making good profits. Some girls had not much more than a cupboard to call their own or shared a room with small children.

Because she became so busy with her small business enterprises, Louie called a young relative from the Philippines to be her personal domestic helper. This girl became mixed up with some nasty types and they reported her to the Immigration Department. 'I was taken to the 14th floor of their building where I was interviewed.' Two officers threatened her and asked about her work in the office but she told them she was looking after an old lady. (Her Taiwan friend's mother.)

They asked to be taken to see this woman. The dear old lady caught on very quickly as to what was happening. She remonstrated with the officers saying that she was blind and needed Louie to help her with everything. She was only pretending and asked Louie to help her with something to demonstrate she couldn't see.

The officers asked if they could see any photos that proved that Louie worked there. 'Get the photo album of my daughter's wedding,' commanded the old woman. Louie was in some of the photos so this convinced them that she was legitimate and they issued the required visa.

But Louie decided that she had had enough of the

deception and decided to leave Hong Kong. She was now working for an immigration officer who probably knew more about her than she realised, so when Louie told her she was leaving, two officers came to fetch her to the airport and stayed with her until she was on the plane for Manila.

Joe was tiring of talking and listening so took a stroll through town and came across the Robinson Mall. The place was crowded with many people who appeared to be window-shopping. He stopped walking for a minute while trying to remember a phone number when he suddenly realised that there was someone standing right next to him. It was a young woman. 'Hullo' he said. She said nothing but looked down. 'And what can I do for you?' Again nothing. 'Can I help you?'

She looked up and quietly said, 'Sir I am looking for a job.'

'Oh, I am sorry, I'm a visitor and have no work to offer you.'

'No, no, sir, that's all right. I have no job, but I am looking for one.'

She held up a large envelope, 'These are my documents for overseas job.'

'I'm sorry but I don't quite understand you.'

'Sir, you come from overseas. What's it like there? I'm going but I'm a bit scared. Please, you tell me about overseas.'

'I don't think I can help you unless you are going to a place I know. Where are you going?'

'I don't know sir, I'm just the applicant.'

'Would you like to tell me about your application? Let me see your papers. Sit down over there and I'll buy us a drink.' It took only a cursory glance for him to see that there was a problem. Some of the documents were photocopied quite roughly, the medical certificate looked distinctly forged. It was. It was a photocopy of an old certificate because he could see the faint outline of a name that had been erased.

He quickly sent a text to Remy 'You had better come and see this.'

Her name was Anna and she had come from a distant village in the province, a product of a very elementary education. The sheer size of Metro Manila had left her gasping. Her family had parted with Ps50,000 with which she applied to an unregistered and therefore illegal recruitment company that had provided the fake documents.

Remy referred the matter to a special government team that investigated illegal recruiters. It only took them ten minutes to come as they had an office nearby. The young woman visibly shook with fear when four husky men surrounded her and began asking questions. They later reported that a ten-minute check revealed the true status of the company. They were working the villages in the south of Anna's province and were known to them. 'We've been on their tail for weeks,' they said, 'and this is the lead we need.'

Joe was sorry not to see the girl again and felt a bit guilty towards her and her family who had worked so hard to raise the money, all to no avail. This has probably left them in serious debt.

He returned to the hotel for some of their really good coffee. Seated opposite him were an elderly man wearing a US navy cap, and an attractive Filipina about 25. CNN was reporting a snowstorm in the Eastern USA. They sat facing each other without speaking. There was something wrong between them. Joe caught his eye and greeted him with, 'Enjoying our nice warm weather? Aren't you glad to be here?'

'Hurrumph, I don't know about that,' said he as he rose from the table and joined Joe. 'I've got my own wintry troubles here.'

'Sorry to hear that. Maybe time will heal it.

'Nothing to do with time. We got married last year,' pointing to the woman who sat with head bowed, 'I gave her family a whole set of furniture last time. Good stuff too. We go back today and its all gone. Everything. What happened? Where is it? Nobody knows. Nobody. These people.' He shrugged his shoulders. 'Who understands them?'

'Perhaps something disastrous has happened in the family so they had to sell it to pay for something, like an operation, maybe the loan shark was after them. There's probably a reasonable explanation but it's too embarrassing to talk about.'

Just at that moment Remy walked in. Joe went to her and quickly asked her to chat with the woman. 'I've asked my friend to have a chat with your wife. It's always easier to talk to a third party.'

'I'm her husband, she talks to me.'

'Yes that's right but here it can be a bit different. I think you will find that there is a reasonable explanation. Whatever it is, I think you will find that your wife deeply respects you and would not want to hurt you in any way. You married into a different culture. I'm sure you have found that out. She probably does so many things quite differently to your first wife. Right now, I can see she is deeply hurt by what has happened.'

Remy returned and explained the problem. They had no sooner left for the States after the wedding when the loan sharks came demanding their money. They knew about the new furniture and demanded they sell it and pay up.

'In a convoluted way you have helped the family out of a severe crisis, and they are grateful but find it very difficult to explain themselves.'

There was time left in the day for Joe to do something that he had wanted to do since coming to Manila, to ride the elevated railway. There were three lines so he bought a ticket to the terminus of the MTR, the Manila Metro Rail System. This one was the line Remy's father helped to clear away many houses that stood in its way. As he sped along EDSA short for Epifano de los Santos Avenue, he marvelled at the amount of vehicular traffic it was supposed to replace. It replaced it all right but with the huge expansion of the city, it was all replaced with even more traffic. 'This will decongest the city's traffic' declared the government when the line opened. But that didn't last long.

After spending time in Asia's largest mall, he took the train back to his hotel at 9 pm. It was so congested that only with an ungentlemanly effort he was able to force himself onto the train. It was so densely packed, that it was impossible to move a limb. And this was the leading car that was reserved for women, children and the elderly. He thought again of the notice at the United Nations Avenue station 'No acts of lasciviousness.' Spelling aside, its message was clear and reminded him of the stories he was told in Tokyo of women being molested in crowded trains.

Rosanna, a second cousin of Remy, came to meet Joe at his hotel. Her story was interesting. 'I have a story for you as does my friend. I am working for a senior Saudi Prince. He is extremely wealthy and I don't know exactly how many servants he has. There are many businesses, racehorses, buildings, houses and palaces all over the world. In fact, I don't know everything about him and his family. I work in one of his palaces and rarely get out of the building. It is completely air-conditioned and this means the air is very dry and neatly all of us have problems with dry skin, sore lips and noses.'

'My work is to teach English and computers to the two children by his third wife. I don't see him very often and when I do, he never speaks to us. His wife though is always here watching over her children. They are both boys so that means they are very important because the other wives have only got daughters.'

'I am very lucky because the two nannies of the boys, they have one each, are both from my village and we went to school together. We are paid good salaries that go straight into our bank accounts. I have a computer with which I teach the boys. They both have iPads. Recently I suggested to my employer that she buy a computer for each of the boys. She agreed immediately and sent someone to buy them. I then suggested she buy one for the nannies too so that all of us can help the boys. To my surprise she took out her phone and called the servant out buying for the maids. All she said was 'buy four not two,' and hung up.'

It was fun to unpack them as we were all so excited.

I also suggested she control how much the boys use them because they are like drugs and children can become addicted to them. She looked at me carefully and said, 'I think you are a very wise woman because I have heard about that problem.' The boys are only 7 and 8 years old and I fear that they will soon know as much as me!

'But my problem is overwork. When I first came here, I asked what day I would have off and the princess looked at me, shocked that I should ask such a question. 'Can I have a day off being a mother? Can you who cares for the boys have a day off? No, no, no days off. This work doesn't stop. The boys don't stop being boys for one day a week! Does the cook take a day off? Of course not. We have to eat every day!' Does the laundry girl have a day off? Of course not, we have to wear clothes every day.' By this time her voice reached screaming level.

'Before I came here, someone told me that the people here think differently to us. I see what they mean now. I read recently where someone has written that the Arab people here have not yet got rid of the idea that they can no longer have slaves and still think that we are like that. But the three of us are very lucky as we have each other, and we are good friends. When the princess is not at home we work together and relieve each other so that we can get a little rest. We share a room and sometimes, when we are alone in our part of the palace, we sing a little song together and pray.'

Rosanna's friend was bursting tell about her employer. 'My employer is very fashion conscious. Even when she leaves the house she is dressed as well as any Muslim woman. Her black gown is far from dowdy. It's made of expensive material and is richly embroidered yet subtly so. Her headscarf sits back on her forehead showing a centimeter of hair that is a lot more than most women. She loves her sandals and has a boot maker come once a month to show the latest styles. He makes all of them for her. One complete wall of her dressing room is lined with shelves of sandals.'

'She has got a whole box of watches this big,' spreading her hands, 'but the one she is proudest of has a strange name, French I think. It's a beautiful gold one covered in diamonds. I have never been able to see all her bangles, but I know they are all gold and some have got diamonds and beautiful green stones. I have seen her bedroom and the many beautiful boxes that her maid said had jewelry in them. They were all locked. I was lucky to be in her room. I would have been in big trouble if she found out.'

'She is only 25 and about 5 feet. Her husband is about 6 feet. She has delicate hands that have never done a day's work, probably can't even make a bed. She has a full-time personal maid from Morocco who bathes her twice day and does her hair and makeup.'

CHAPTER ELEVEN

'I think we should start with Oman. This will be an easy country for you to work in,' said the controller, 'at least for starters. We have large numbers of people there and they are easily contacted especially the Christians. The government, recognising the need for churches to exist, has provided compounds where churches are allowed to operate. All you have to do is to turn up on a Saturday, their holy day, and you will find more people than you could possibly speak to. Don't go on Sundays, there will be none there.'

'First of all, take a few days off and see something of our beautiful islands. Remy, take him to Cebu or Bicol, there's plenty to see and do.' She delivered him to the Sulo Hotel promising to call him next morning.

'Here's tickets for Bicol region. We leave at midday,' announced Remy next morning. However, there was a problem. One of the frequent typhoons that hit the Philippines every year had just knocked the city around. The airport was relatively intact but the devastation wreaked on the nearby houses was dreadful. The typhoon had only just cleared the area before the plane was allowed to land at sunset so there had hardly been time to commence the cleaning up process. There was only one taxi at the airport. All roads had been blocked by fallen trees and washouts. It could take them to the only hotel accessible. This was a small two-floor establishment that wouldn't deserve even a single star rating. It was only a few hundred metres away. The receptionist gave them a warm welcome, then dropped he eyes to murmur, 'Sorry, but we only have one room.' Then looked up smiling, 'but it's got a double bed. There's a new mattress. It was put on last night. We have sold all our other rooms to a Japanese tour group that is stranded here.

'We need two rooms,' said Remy, 'we're not married, just work mates.'

'Where's the old mattress,' said Joe, 'put it on the floor and I'll sleep on that.'

The owner walked in at that moment and heard the last comment. 'Well, it is an emergency situation, I suppose we can do that.'

Next morning from the upstairs room all they could see was the destruction that had happened just hours before. The typhoon was unusual for these parts in that it was quite narrow. It had cut a path very close to the hotel and amazingly had swung around it on three sides. Leaving the hotel building intact but flattening dozens of houses.

'I'm not sure why we are here,' said Joe next morning. 'What can we do and see here? All I know about this place is in this brochure. It describes the whale fish. You know, I like the décor here. It's all made of rope.

'That's because its our famous hemp fibre. Its exported all over the world.'

Their pretty waitress overheard the comment and said, 'my brother can take you to see the *butanding*. He loves them. He's right here because he's our hotel guide. Well not really, he just loves to tell people about or place.'

'Thanks,' said Joe, 'but this is not the time to be a tourist. What can we do to help people who got caught by the typhoon?'

'The government will help them. We have a special department for natural disasters because we get so many,' said Remy.

By this time a small group had gathered around them including some hotel staff and the tour leader of the Japanese group who said, 'I am sure that all of my people will want to help too. I'll collect some money from them and we can buy things for the people.'

Pointing out the window down what was left of the street the manager said, 'The only shop we have here is almost gone, but maybe the owner can sell what is left of his goods.'

Fifty-kilo bags of rice, too heavy to be blown away were about all he had left along with a few cartons of tinned goods. They had a quick consultation with the hotel owner and quickly agreed to pay the shop owner for his entire stock and then told him to give it all away freely to the people around him. Later when Joe tallied up figures he said to the Japanese, 'that cost each of us the price of two good meals.'

Later that day after a path had been cleared the taxi took them to see the famous whale fish. Joe was amazed at the narrow path of the typhoon; it was only about 100 metres wide. It had come in from the sea in the East, did a semicircle around the hotel and back the way it had come. Their guide hired a small boat and within minutes they came across the world's largest fish swimming just below the surface. 'They can grow to 40 feet but this one is only about 35,' enthused the guide. 'Our waters are their home and there are more here than anywhere else in the world.'

They found another hotel in the city and moved in next day. The room maid was in his room after returning from breakfast and he surprised her standing in the bathroom sniffing loudly. She quickly dried her face and with red puffy eyes began to apologise. 'What's the matter?'

'I have got a text from my husband. He's lost his job. He's in Saudi so he's coming home.'

'Then why the tears, aren't won't you be happy to see him?'

'Of course I will, but he's supposed to be earning so that the children can go to high school.'

'Tell me all about it,' said Joe sitting on the bed.

It was the usual story of a father being willing to work overseas in order to help the family. Although relatively unskilled except for his driver's licence, he was able to find work in Saudi that brought in more money that he could ever hope to earn in Bicol. 'One month there is like one year here. He's only had three months.' She went on to say that the plan was that after he had done one contract of two years, she would go for two years working as a nanny or domestic helper. She was sad that he had to come home so soon and scared of the prospect of her going away.

Joe decided that he would like three days of rest and recreation in the luxury hotel while Remy went off to visit her family in another part of the province. 'I'm not going to tour around, I'm going to eat, read and sleep and not talk to anyone,' he declared as he saw Remy off on the bus. Four days later, she turned up with tickets for Manila. He put the envelope in his pocket asking, 'What time do we leave?'

'Tonight but look at them. They are for the train not the plane.

'Train? You, beauty.'

'Oh I'm beautiful am I?'

'Yes you are but at home, that's what we call someone who has done something nice.'

'You are going to love this one. It's even got a deluxe toilet.'

That was a strange thing to say thought Joe, but this was the Mayon deluxe express to Manila. A private compartment had been booked. The toilet was indeed something special in that it comprised two rooms, one for the plumbing and another for a lady to do her toilette that included a padded chair before a mirror.

After a comfortable night they were awakened by the regular blowing of the locomotive horn as it threaded its way through the crowded markets that encroached onto the railway line leading into Manila.

OMAN

Obtaining a visa for Oman was quite different from anything he had experienced. A confirmed booking at an international hotel was all that was needed, as the hotel would officially sponsor him. A quick phone call to a local Filipina pastor provided the information needed.

The immigration officer dealing with him in an attempt to be friendly said, 'You come for job?'

'No, no. I'm just a tourist. I like to see Oman not work here.'

'But you must see the job. It is here. Very interesting for you.'

'Thank you but no, I can't work here is this not just a tourist visa?'

'No, no, not working just job, you know job?'

Deep in the recesses of the mind Joe suddenly remembered reading something about the tomb of Job of the Bible. 'Oh, you mean Jobe, Joab. Nabi Job? The prophet Job. Then remembering the name in Indonesian that was probably Arabic, and said, Oh Ayub?'

'Ah yes, the Nabi Ayub, Job. You must see.'

A few minutes later while waiting at the luggage carousel the same immigration officer came to him and handing a card said, 'This my name. You please come to my house, we drink coffee and we go to see Nabi Job.'

Next day a car came for Joe and after picking up his host at the airport drove to his house. Seated in a spacious room furnished only with large cushions and fine animal skins and rugs, they drank traditional coffee, hot and sweet. There was no sign of any other people. The coffee was already set out when they entered the room and when it was time for a refill, his host, Abdul, clapped his hands and a young woman appeared with an elegant silver coffeepot. Joe instantly recognised her to be a Filipina. He greeted her in Tagalog and was so taken aback she nearly dropped it.

Far from being angry with him for speaking to a woman servant, Abdul said, 'You speak her language? Go ahead talk some more.'

Joe was limited to asking her name and how she was. Sinking quickly to her knees she answered quietly, then nodding to her employer left the room. They talked about families and work and the good government Oman enjoyed under the Sultan.

Muslims recognise Job as a prophet, hence the title Nabi Job. He is mentioned a couple of times in the Quran. His traditional tomb was cared for very well and painted in a green and white. It was in a remarkable good condition seeing that he lived around 2000 BC! Near a mosque is a gold domed shrine that contains the tomb of Job (Ayoub) in a large room. It is surrounded by a green carpet and a few prayer mats. Overhead is a beautiful glass chandelier.

Reading up about him later, Joe discovered that there is another tomb for Job in Turkey but that's best not mentioned in Oman, which incidentally, considers itself to be one of the Christian holy lands (along with Israel, Lebanon, Jordan, Turkey and Syria).

On the way home Abdul stopped at the famous frankincense tree orchard. Like apples, there are many types of frankincense trees but according to Abdul, this one here in this place was the very one the wise men used to make a gift for the baby Jesus. At least that is what he thought he meant because his English was appalling. The tree is tapped for it's white resin.

On Friday Joe turned up at one of the church compounds to find a variety of buildings that house more than twenty-five different church groups. At six a.m. he met with the pastors of these churches at their regular monthly meeting and they described the religious freedom they have, so long as their activities were confined to this compound. Although a Muslim, the Sultan believes that every individual ought to have the right to worship in the way that he chooses and the people of all faiths are provided with facilities to do this. He follows the Ibadhi 'denomination' of Islam (one of about 200) known for its moderate conservatism There are four specially designated Christian compounds in the capital city in four of the main suburbs. Two of these are quite large in area and accommodate several church buildings. Two have been in existence for over 100 years.

There are 6,000 expatriate protestant Christians in Muscat, the capital of Oman, and another 6,000 in the interior of the country. These would be figures for nominal Christians, in other words any person coming from the Philippines would be regarded as a Christian. One out of five is a practising, Christian. There are 10,000-12,000 Roman Catholic believers.

Sixty percent of the population of the country was made up of foreign workers occupying positions from paediatric neurosurgeons to street sweepers. The church services were held in twelve languages including many of the Philippines. There were five Filipino pastors who were only too ready to describe the conditions some of their people faced. Most people were well cared for by their employers but there were a few who caused endless trouble. One pastor pled with him to visit work camps in desert areas where the conditions for some of the men were not good. 'Maybe we have to leave that for another time, but my brief is to look into the needs of the womenfolk.'

A spokesman for the pastors said 'generally speaking the people of the Middle East do not respect Asians. Attitudes to servants vary greatly from those who regard them as part of the family to people who have no rights: they are workers no more no less. As such, they have no rights; their position in life is to serve their masters without question. If they are Christians then their position can be even worse because they are unbelievers, kaffirs, the lowest of the low because they do not believe in Muhammad. As far as some fundamental Muslim believers are concerned, they hardly deserve to live while they in rejection of Muhammad. Some take the Koran at its word when it states that if a person will not accept Mohammad, he doesn't deserve to live such as this verse: Q. 9: 123mOh ye who believe! Murder those of the disbelievers and let them find harshness (qilzat) in you.

'Many of the people are house maids and they are at the beck and call of their people all the time, and for some even sexual pressure as well as loneliness and frustration. One of the problems is that these girls are not free to leave their families because many of them are not allowed out of the household; sometimes this is because the sponsors feel for their safety.

'Stay with me and I'll introduce you to some of the women leaders. We always share a meal after our service so there's plenty of time to talk.'

The first person he saw outside the church was the young woman, Melissa, who worked for the immigration officer, Abdul. She rushed over to Joe warmly greeting him and happily telling her friend that she had served him coffee in the house. Claiming him as her friend she insisted on sitting with him in the church and escorted him to the communal lunch after the service. This was a very special occasion for workers all so far away from home and Joe loved the sound of a couple of hundred happy voices enjoying 'the fellowship.'

He spotted a dozen men in one corner and went to speak with them. They were all service workers of some sort and one fellow who said he was 'the physiotherapist to the royal family and their staff.'

A pastor explained, 'When people are living in a foreign country they tend to mix with people from their homeland. There are large numbers of Christians among the expatriate workers in Oman and as a result of meeting so many Christian Filipinas many, of whom were only nominal Christians when they first came to Oman, have become practising Christians.'

The pastor said that the secret of the blessing that God has given his small church lay in the fact that they promote the Bible. He said 'The Bible is an important part of our outreach to our fellow countrymen among whom we live and work. There are so few books here that it is the only book many of them read and we find that when people read the Bible carefully, they find God. As they read it, and along with the testimony of their compatriots who are living by the Bible, they are attracted to the real truth of Christianity. A great number of these people have been nominal Christians all their lives but on being faced with the challenge of reading God's word have become practicing Christians. The fact is that many don't have any entertainment, no radio or TV and few books so they have plenty of time to spend reading the Bible.

'But behind all this is the fact that because so many work very hard with little time off, and some are never allowed out of their apartment, all they have is the Bible. We are lucky in Oman, because we are allowed to bring our Bibles into the country. You can't do that in Saudi Arabia.'

A bright-faced woman was keen to speak with Joe. 'When I came to Oman seven years ago to work as a domestic helper for an Omani family, it was not possible to attend a church service. My employers, who were always very kind to me, would not let me leave the house, so I had to work every day for the two years. They said that it was not safe for me to be going out alone.'

'Do you really mean working every day for two years without a day off?'

'Yes I do, it was every day.'

'And yet you say they were always very kind to you? How can that be, making you work every day?'

'But sir, don't you realise that servants here are servants. We have no rights. We do everything they tell us to do.

'During this time, I was often feeling very homesick and lonely because it was not possible to spend much time with other people and certainly there was no way that I could get to Church. I found that the only thing that I had to keep my faith alive and strong was my Bible. I used to spend any spare time that I had reading the Bible and, of course, writing letters home, but it was God's word that I fed on constantly which kept me walking close to God.' Because I spend so much time reading my Bible, I learned so much and it was a great help to me.

'I renewed my contract for another two years and at this time my employer decided to give me two days off per month. This was every second Friday so that it would be possible for me to attend a Christian church service.

'After completing four years with this family I decided to renew my contract for another two, and so during this third period they allowed me to have three Fridays off per month. This meant that I was able to spend much more time with my Christian friends and to be able to enjoy rich fellowship with them.'

Joe was at the airport departure lounge waiting for a flight to Bahrain when a young Filipina began speaking with him. Her experience as a maid interested him greatly as it was an entirely different story.

Kept locked up in the apartment for months on end she desperately tried to find some form of relaxation. She was not allowed a telephone; the one in the family flat was fitted with a special dialling lock. There was neither TV nor DVD player, no books, newspapers nor magazines. I had a radio for a while until the batteries wore out but they refused to buy me more. But she had a Bible. 'I was never allowed to go to church but I discovered that by going up to the roof at night, I could see the stars and think about God. I found these verses in Isaiah 'With my own hand I created the earth and stretched out the sky. They obey my every command.' (Isa 48 v13)

Actually, when I came here, I was a Christian but I wasn't serious about my faith. But watching my employer praying every day was a challenge to me. She would put on a special gown that reached from neck to toes. The she put on a funny looking hat that was like an old-fashioned granny hat, the sort they used to wear to bed. It had frilly edges and a drawstring to pull it tight around her face. She was so serious about this, and she didn't mind if I saw her praying.

'One day I showed her my Bible especially the verse about God making the stars. This annoyed her very much and screamed at me, "Put that away. That's a filthy book. I don't want ever to see it again. Hide it from me if you want to keep it. If I see it again, I will destroy it."

'That was a terrible day for me, one moment I was challenged to see her faith and perseverance and the next I was horribly condemned for my own faith and for reading God's book.'

Joe withdrew to the side of the room and sat and

watched the crowd of about one hundred people enjoying themselves. They were mostly women with a sprinkling of men all from the Philippines. Then he noticed a woman sitting by herself a picture of desolation. Joe went and sat down beside her, greeting her with a bright, 'hullo. How are you?' Where do you come from?'

She turned to him, her eyes red from crying, 'well sir, I'm from Cebu and I'm not happy like these people. Look at them sir, they are all far away from home yet they look so happy and enjoying themselves. I am wondering why they are so happy. I'm not happy, why are they?'

'Do you belong to this church? Are you a member?'

'No sir, I'm a Catholic and these are all Protestants.'

'Aren't Catholics happy too?'

'Yes of course sir, but not like this. When I go to our church, we are also happy to see each other but there is something different here. I don't understand it.'

'Do you now the expression 'the joy of the Lord?'

'Er, I don't think so. What is it?'

'Well, the Bible teaches that when a person becomes a real Christian, her heart is filled with joy because she knows her sins are forgiven and that she has been given eternal life. That's called the joy of the Lord. I think you will find that nearly all these people here are practising Christians and therefore they are very happy within themselves, not just because they have a day off.'

At that moment Pastor Bayong came along so Joe said, 'Pastor have a talk with this lady, I think she needs to know how she too can be filled with the joy of the Lord. You had better explain it in Cebuano because that's her language and yours too.'

'Would you like you come to our filfel tonight? Asked Melissa. 'Filfel that sounds interesting. What is it? No, let me guess, it's the Filipina Fellowship. Right?' About 30 met together for supper and fellowship. They crowded around Joe eager to talk and ask him questions about his visit. He didn't let on the real reason but asked them what it was like for them to work in Oman. Most of them were eager to tell of their work and how much they loved being there. 'Today of course is our special day,' said one. We go to church in the morning, shop in the afternoon and fellowship in the evening.'

'You didn't say when you talk together,' joked Joe. 'I think talking together is very important today.'

'That's fellowship.'

'Yes, but do you know the basic meaning of fellowship. It means 'all the fellows together in the same ship.' Ships sail through calm waters, rough waters, storms, sometimes they are becalmed.' What's it really like working here in Oman?'

'Ah, in all our experiences here we have each other. If someone has a problem, we call each other.'

'What sort of problems do you have?'

They all laughed. 'Every sort here. Like how to make something, or how to take out a burn mark when we are ironing.'

One said, 'my maam saw a Pavlova desert in a magazine and told me to make one. I've never seen one let alone make one. My friend works for a New Zealand family so I called her and she told me.'

'Was it a success?'

'It tasted ok but didn't seem to be big enough.'

They closed their meeting with a couple of songs. One was a traditional Philippine folk song then a Christian one called 'God be with you 'till we meet again.'

As he was preparing to leave a couple of women, more perspicacious than the rest, asked 'Why did you really come here?'

'Can we met somewhere quiet where we can talk privately?' One took him by the hand and led him to a side room in the church where Joe quietly explained his mission. They looked very grave and said, 'we know that this is a great need. Here in Oman it's rare for us to be treated badly but over there,' waving her hand toward Saudi, 'we have heard stories.'

Jeana the said, 'You had better hear my story. I did a term in Saudi Arabia and one day when I was cooking, I was tasting the food when my employer came into the kitchen. She saw me and yelled, 'That's not your food. That's ours. Don't you dare eat it.'

'But maam, I'm only tasting it to get it right.'

'You don't taste it.'

'But maam, I'm a trained chef. We were always taught to taste the food as we cook: it's important to get it right.'

'You don't taste anything here,' she yelled.

'At that moment her husband came and she screamed, 'She's been eating our food.' He stepped up to me and took me by the hair and shook me and said, 'Get out, you don't eat our food.'

'I threw down the spoon onto the floor and ducked around him and went to my room. He followed me and once again grabbed my hair and shook me and said, 'You eat what we give you.'

'Ok sir, but don't blame me if it's not salty or too hot.' He let go of my hair and punched me in the stomach. I fell down grasping for air. He went out and slammed the door swearing in Arabic.

'The next day the maid, who was serving the food and

could speak a bit of Arabic, told me that she thought they were complaining to each other about the food having no salt. 'That's right, there's not enough. I know. Don't worry the next one will be too hot.'

'There was an extra spoon of chilli powder in the biryani and they were soon yelling from the table in anger. The maam came storming into the kitchen and slammed down the dish on the counter. 'This is too hot, its burning us. The master is yelling at me.'

'Sorry maam, but how can I tell, I can't taste it first can I? I will make another one.'

'This maam could not cook anything. I never even saw her make a cup of tea. What went on in the kitchen was a mystery to her. So very quietly I said to her, 'Don't worry maam, just let me do my job and everything will be all right. There's something else in the fridge that you can have.' My quiet tone soothed her and with a grateful look, left me to it.

'I always cooked the main course a day ahead so that there was always something I could pull out if there were unexpected guests. I had prepared a delicious lamb stew. Even though I made it myself, it really is a delicious stew because the recipe was given to me by a friend who is in a prince's kitchen. Ten minutes later I sent it out and listening at the door, I could hear sounds of appreciation. The serving maid said, 'Oh they like that one.'

'Later that evening, the maam came to me and in the only display of gratitude she had ever shown me, touched my shoulder and said very quietly, 'Thank you. Everything is ok. I'm sorry he hit you.' I took that to mean that I could continue to taste the food I cooked.

'I was so overcome with gratitude that I whispered, "Thank you Jesus."

'What did you say? Was it Jesus? You mean Isa?'

'Yes maam, you know that I am a Christian, I follow Isa.'

'But tell me why you talk to him like that?'

'Our holy book tells us we can talk to him at any time. He's with me now, all the time.'

'Mmmm I don't think you can do that. If you want to pray to God you have to get dressed first and kneel on your rug in the right way.'

'Well, maam, all you can do is to follow what your holy book says. Just like I do. I follow the Injil that God gave to Isa, just like your book says.'

That started a heated discussion with her saying that Isa is not the true prophet, Mohammad is. The Saudi government would not let me bring my Bible so I had an English Koran and read it quite a bit. I could find some things I liked and I knew the place where it says 'we caused Jesus the son of Mary to follow them, and we gave him the evangel...'

'I didn't know that. I'll have to check that out.'

'A few days later when we were alone in the house, she came to me and said, 'I want you to tell me about your beliefs. I can see they make you a nice person.'

'Thanks maam, but I'm not nice, it's the spirit if Jesus that makes me nice.'

'We talked for hours and then the next day. I didn't have a computer but I heard that you could now get the Bible online so suggested she try it.

'About a week later, when her husband had gone away on a business trip, she came to me and said, 'You are now my sister,' and threw her arms around me and wept. How could this be? That she would call her servant a sister? She then explained that she had spent many hours on the computer reading the Bible. I had noticed that she had been spending a lot of time alone on her bedroom.

'It was a very serious thing for a Muslim woman to convert to Christianity. The Koran calls for her death if she does not renounce her newfound faith. There was every likelihood that her husband would denounce her and report her to the Sharia law authorities. Family life as she had known it would be finished. Going into hiding with other Christians was a possibility but not without the right contacts.

'What am I going to do,' she wailed hugging Juliana tightly.

'I think that you do nothing maam.'

'I'm your sister now not your maam. At least in private call me Fatima.'

'Please, do nothing, say nothing. Just treasure Jesus in your heart. When you pray, pray to him not Muhammad. No one will know.' I was then able to explain that I came from the southern Philippines where there are many Muslims. I know Christians there who look like Muslims.

'There is a place in the Bible that explains to women like her what to do. I Peter 3 v 1 & 2. So I asked her to let me find it on the computer and read it to her and explained that when her husband sees what a change has taken place in her life he will begin to wonder what has happened to her. She won't have to say anything. Like Peter wrote, 'If you are a wife, you must put your husband first. Even if he opposes our message, you will win him over by what you do. No one else will have to say anything to him because he will see how you honour God and live a pure life. Don't depend on fancy hairdos or gold jewellery or expensive clothes to make you look beautiful. Be beautiful in your heart, by being gentle and quiet. This kind of beauty will last and God considers it very special.'

'The lady couldn't understand how would it be that she would change? I just said, 'Look what has happened just now. Your attitude to me has changed so much. I can see in your face a joy that wasn't there before. You can't hide the pleasure that suddenly you know that because you believed in Isa, your sins have been forgiven, they are gone. You don't have to go to the mosque or put on your gown to pray again for your sins to go.'

Joe was at the airport departure lounge waiting for a flight to Bahrain when a young Filipina began speaking with him. By the time she had finished her story several others had gathered around and some were keen to talk to Joe but a boarding call ended their chat.

Joe's flight was delayed two hours and he was soon in conversation with three well-dressed young Filipina women. They had just come in from Saudi and were to transfer to a flight for London. They worked for a Saudi prince, part of a team of six who served him and his princess wife. They explained the roles they had. One was the personal maid to the princess and was required to be within calling distance 24/7. The other was her beautician who bathed her every morning and night and attended to her hair and makeup. Another was the wardrobe mistress who also did the laundry and ironing for the couple. Nearby were another small group. They were the prince's staff consisting of a secretary, a personal maid, and a masseuse who was also responsible for the luggage when travelling.

'Where are they?' asked Joe looking around.

'They are in a private plane with their uncle. We will meet up in London at their apartment.'

'Sounds like you all have good jobs.'

'Oh yes,' they chorused, 'we do. When we get to London, we will have a holiday because there are people there who will do all the work.'

'London's expensive.'

'No problem, she's got the credit card,' pointing to the

secretary. 'The prince pays for everything.' As Joe left them, they all took out their brand-new iPhones supplied by the prince and began helping each other to use them.

CONVERSION FROM ISLAM

Joe's plane was delayed again for several hours and for the first time ever was pleased about it because it gave him time to talk to other workers. He met Guadeloupe whom he found sitting alone weeping silently. He gingerly approached her and asked what was wrong. He began with 'Are you missing your family terribly?'

'No, no sir, it's my Saudi family and began weeping with great intensity. Although making hardly any sound her body shook with emotion. I've been thrown out of Saudi Arabia because I'm a Christian and my employers have become Christians and they have taken them away. I think they are dead now. They were secret Christian believers.'

It took many minutes for her to calm down. Finally, she dried her tears and told her story. The maid before she was a strong Christian whose life and testimony before her Saudi family was such that they began to ask questions about her life. They could see that she was different, always working well and in a good spirit. When she received the news that both her parents had died in a boating accident, her reaction was completely different to what they expected. Although sorely grieved at receiving the news weeks after the event had happened, she took it with such grace that they began to wonder about her.

One evening they called her to them and asked what it was that helped her to accept the bad news with such grace and acceptance. The maid sank to her knees and explained her Christian faith. That her parents were both in God's hands and that they knew they had eternal salvation and had been forgiven of their sins. Taking an enormous risk, she asked their permission to get her Bible and read to them about this. She had smuggled the Bible into the country and if she had been found out the consequences could have been disastrous.

For an hour she read relevant passages and the family listening closely. 'We had no idea that the Bible was like that.' The result was that her employers decided that the Bible was the true revelation from God and were prepared to accept its message. But to confess to family and friends that they had become Christian believers because they now believed that Isa (Jesus) was the true Saviour of the world and not Mohammad would have meant imprisonment, perhaps exile or worse, torture or death. They continued to appear to be Muslims on the outside but when in the mosque, they were praying in the name of Jesus. They borrowed the maid's Bible and sometimes read it together with her.

When Guadeloupe came, she couldn't understand the family. They seemed to me a strange mix of Islam and Christian but she dared not say anything. One day while cleaning a cupboard when the family were out, she found the former maid's Bible. It was wrapped up in a beautiful cloth. She had not brought her own Bible knowing that it was forbidden, so she very excitedly began to read some of her favourite chapters. So engrossed in reading, she did not hear the family return and was startled when her employer came into the room and found her. Quickly she said, 'No it's quite all right, you can read it. We like to read it too.'

That evening she was called to speak with the family and they explained their secret conversion. It didn't take much to convince Guadeloupe to keep the secret and they soon began to have Bible readings together. In an open and frank way, they discussed the question of what to teach their twin children. They were still of preschool age. Then the maid had a brilliant idea. Many of the people and the stories of the Bible are also found in the Koran. Why should she not read them the stories from the Koran and the Bible and this way they would learn both religions? This seemed to be ok for about a year but when their teachers began to notice that they knew more about the Koran characters than usual because the Bible accounts are much longer with more detail that the Koran, they began to ask them many questions. The religious police were alerted and they came to question the parents. It didn't take them very long to discover the truth. The religious police came to the house and arrested us all. The government department that deals with children of convicted criminals took them away. They found them in the bedroom, wrapped them in blankets and removed them without even allowing the parents to say good-bye. The parents were then handcuffed and led away.

Guadeloupe had difficulty in describing the rest of the story. She was given five minutes to pack her things, taken to the airport and put on the first plane to leave the country. This was in Bahrain, where miraculously she was admitted and permitted to work without the usual formalities. Her employers, 'Mohamed and Asri, were separated and I do not know what happened to them.'

But Joe knew that it is against the law to convert and it is likely that, if they did not recant their Christian faith, they will be killed in some way, perhaps beheaded, and that possibly after unspeakable torture.

Guadeloupe had been told to wait at the airport while a visa was arranged for her. 'You can buy a Bible here at the airport. Go to the small bookshop over there they have English and Tagalog Bibles.' She brightened at that and even wept some more when Joe offered to buy one for her.

'Oh what can I say. Thank you, sir. You see I don't have much money because they didn't pay me. Well, they couldn't, the police grabbed them and took them away giving them no chance to do anything.

'Oh sir, what can I do? I'm the one who taught the children so it's all my fault. Do you think they will be alright?' She bent down, head on knees and sobbed uncontrollably. Joe sat there wanting to console her but not knowing what to do. I can't touch her he thought, this is a Muslim place. Then suddenly he realised that he was not officially in the country but on the airside. He placed his arms around her and hugged her lightly. 'The children will be fine. They will probably go to a foster family or to a government orphanage. Who knows, they might get another Christian nanny. You can still pray for them. But it is against the law to convert so we'll have to pray that their lives will be spared and not made to suffer too much.' The government there does not hide the fact that their law states very clearly that people who convert then refuse to recant will die. 'Remember your family made the choice to convert even before you met them. Your time with them doubtless strengthened their faith so that will help them now.'

CHAPTER TWELVE

Joe was back in Manila for meetings with the authorities regarding problems with the OFW. He was quite astounded at the way they received him, with such great dignity and honour. He was introduced as 'a friend of our people, willing to take risks for us.' Given the chance to address the meeting Joe outlined the world history of house servants and in particular live-in maids. Even the most casual reading of literature reveals the fact that there have always been problems with this. Many of the most aristocratic families of Europe and the UK admit to the abuse of female servants. There is many a story of indiscretions. Even some of the mullato populations of the American countries can be traced back to employers taking advantage of black or brown servants and slaves.

There were even a couple of USA presidents who were accused of fathering illegitimate children by their maids and stories are numerous regarding the British royal family of old and other royal families of Europe.

They had more than a casual interest in the statement he made regarding the history of the English in the periodical 'The Daily Mash.' (Whether it was true or not he didn't know). Under the heading 'One in five descended from bastard children of scullery maids.' According to Professor Henry Brubaker of the Institute for Studies, 'Basically your great-great-great grandmother was dragged into a stable and ravished or traded her virtue for a boiled sweet.' 30th July 2012.

'Look at this, Al Arabiya News' of 1st Feb 2011 issued a report entitled 'Three million maids abused in Arab world.' This was according to a survey by the Saudi magazine Sayidaty.

'Islamic law and practices over the centuries have made it easy for some modern-day Arabs to believe they have the right of access to their female servants as in the days of slavery, the maid was simply a possession, not a woman.'

My purpose today is not to excuse the perpetrators of this practise but perhaps help us understand how this modern day situation has developed. Recent laws of protecting human rights should correct this injustice.

'But I have noticed that even here in this county house servant, although they are called helpers, are treated differently. If I visited you in your home, would you introduce me to your children and to any relatives that might be in the house? Yes, you would. Would you introduce me to the servants, the helpers? No, you probably wouldn't. Why not? They possibly live with you; they are almost part of the family.'

He looked around the group. Heads bowed, no one said a word. 'I think I can say that you treat them humanely, but they are not really family, they are servants. I was in the home of a very respectable family the other night. They have a three-story house and two maids and a cook served us a beautiful meal. I was not introduced to them, but as I was leaving, the three of them stood together to smile at me as I left. I thanked them for the lovely meal. Their response was heartening but my host gave a laugh of embarrassment. The sort of reaction that seemed to say 'you didn't have to do that.'

'In the case of non-Christian communities such as Shintoism, Buddhism and Muslim countries, the Christian ethic does not exist. Christ taught that the greatest commandment was to love God and the second one was to love our neighbour. Loving, or respecting other people is ingrained in our culture. This is one of the greatest difficulties your people have when they live and work with non-Christian families.

'Let me tell you a true story of a friend, who with several others, drove a car from England to India. When passing through a country in the Middle East they ran over a young girl. She had darted across the road in front of the vehicle and was badly injured. The police arrested them, both driver and passengers, and charged them all for dangerous driving. They all appeared before a magistrate but, believing the witnesses, discharged the case as it clearly was not their fault. Immediately on leaving the court, the group went to visit the child in hospital and took a small gift. The police observing this, immediately re-arrested them all saying, "that you came to visit the girl clearly shows you know you are guilty." To them, all the people in the car were accountable, not just the driver. The idea of Christian compassion was not understood.

'But remember one of the basic tenants of the Muslim faith is to give to the poor and needy but that is not done in the Christian way that is based on love. To many Muslims it's merely a duty. You see this all over the world, they will throw a coin to a beggar but not help him in any way. Of course, there are exceptions to this, but the Koran does not teach 'love your neighbour' in the same way as the Bible does.'

Placing a large file on the table Joe said, 'Here are the details of the people I have interviewed, including their contracts, employment agencies and the people they work for. There is some information missing that I was not able to get.'

Next morning Joe went for coffee at the nearby French Coffee Shop. Sitting on a stool on the pavement outside was a young girl carefully pulling out her under arm hair one by one. In the café a man was calling a person on his mobile phone. In a loud voice he was castigating someone for not sending him the US$500 that he had requested. In a loud voice he instructed the person to send the money through Western Union. All the staff was laughing and commenting on him, embarrassed at such behaviour in their shop. He knew enough Tagalog to realize that something was wrong so asked the waitress. She shrugged her shoulders and said, 'His daughter is overseas and is not sending the money he wants.'

He went walking back to the hotel and a taxi driver who always seemed to be there asked him about his plans offering to take him 'anywhere, see anything, meet any one, buy anything, shopping, post office, bank, swimming, massage, drinking, old city, new city, drugging, sightseeing, boys, girls, women, men, cathedral, churches...anything you like..' it was quite a professional spiel covering the entire gamut of all possible tourist activities.

'Thanks, but maybe tomorrow,' trying to slip away without having to talk. But next day he was at it again. 'Ok, how much for one hour sightseeing? How much?' They quickly agreed on a price and set off into the dense morning traffic. At the first traffic light stop the driver took up his phone and hurriedly said what Joe later thought was 'Ok, I've got him' followed by a stream of Tagalog or at least something that sounded a bit like it. The number of the taxi and name of the driver was displayed prominently so he had the presence of mind to make a note of them.

They were soon into the depths of small side streets of old Manila when he suddenly stopped outside an old warehouse. One toot of the horn and the doors swung open and he drove in, the doors clanging shut behind him. Before Joe could utter a word of protest or alarm, the car doors were opened and he was roughly pulled out, slammed to the ground, and someone quickly tied a thick black towel around his head effectively blindfolding him. Then another was tied over his mouth gagging him. He was lifted to his feet and frogmarched into a side room where, with a rough push, he was pitched forward onto the floor and the door slammed shut. His head hit the leg of a steel table and before he could recover from that, the door opened and someone came in pulled him to his feet and bound his hands together behind him, then kneed him in the back to send him sprawling across the floor.

Ten minutes later a man came in and kicked him savagely in the head that laid him out cold. He was just coming to when a couple of thugs untied his bonds and put him into the taxi and took him to another address. Two men walked beside him acting as though he was either very sick or drunk. They threw him onto a bed, tied him up and punched him on the side of the head and left him. A few hours later as he struggled into consciousness, he heard a soft voice in his ear, 'Wake up mister it's time to talk.' He found himself on a bed in a small unpainted room. He was lying on his back with his arms tied at the wrists and fasted to his belt at the front. His blindfold and gag had been pulled down to his neck. The voice whispered in his ear then soft lips kissed his cheek. 'What are you wanting sir? Why are you here?' He couldn't see close up without glasses but he could make out the face of a woman. 'We're sorry to make you sleep like that but I can help you. Just tell me what you want.'

'Who are you? Are you the wife of the thug who hit me?'

'Ha ha, not his wife, just his woman. We are protecting our people and we want to know why you are asking so many questions.' She drew back and with his eyes focussing properly he could see that she was a good-looking woman but with almond shaped hard steely eyes. Chinese maybe.

It was immediately apparent to Joe that he was being held by a group who operated hiring scams and they didn't want him disturbed their operation.

For ten minutes she talked and tried to coax him to speak. She whispered in his ear, then kissed it, then touched his hands then held his fingers squeezing and stroking them, all the time assuring him that he would not come to any harm if he would just tell them what he was doing, and who he worked for.

Two men came into the room and yelled to the woman to leave. One picked him up off the bed and stood him on the floor and the other landed two heavy punches to the solar plexus, a right and a left, Joe doubled up in pain and they threw him back on the bed and left, slamming the door, calling, 'when we come back you talk.'

They left him alone all day until at about sunset when the door rattled open and an empty plastic bucket and one filled with water as well as a tray was placed inside the room. There was a can of coke, a glass of water and a plate of instant noodles. For three days that was the only thing that happened, the same food and drink once a day. The bucket served as the toilet and was not emptied. Constricted by his bindings it took a long time to eat and drink as his arms allowed little movement.

The plan was that Joe would meet up with Remy and Rico in the morning so it wasn't until ten o'clock that they began to wonder what had happened to him. He was not at the hotel and they waited all day. Next morning the hotel reported that he had not slept in his room that night neither had he eaten or drunk at their restaurant or bar. By midday they had become quite worried so Rico called his police cousin at headquarters.

The police commander called his team of detectives together and after providing the description sent them out to look for Joe. He was not in any hospital. They had no idea where to look but they were told that he was probably being held by an underworld gang. 'Check up on all their known hideouts,' they were told.

On the fifth day Joe woke to a noise and scuffling outside his door. There was an argument that he took to be about a cell phone. He turned over and tried to sleep. Then he heard a beep that occurred several times a day. He suddenly recognized that it was a cell phone signalling that it was now charged up. It was somewhere in the room. He struggled off the bed and with tiny steps of just a few inches each he managed despite his bindings, to cross the floor and under an old coat lying on the floor he found a cell phone charging. Hey, he thought, that's what the argument was about. With his hands tied together to his belt, it was with great difficulty he managed to turn it on the and then consider what was the local emergency number. Was it 999, 111 or 112, or 123? This place follows America he thought so perhaps they use 112. He pressed the numerals then knelt down to listen. The operator answered immediately. He quickly explained his problem but the operator said, 'Sorry sir, I can't understand you.'

'Please tell the police I have been kidnapped and I think I am in a house. 'I'm an Americano. Tell Remy Bernardo and her boss Rico that I'm here. Do you understand? Americano, kidnapped.

Despite her questions he couldn't tell her the official name of the organization or whom Rico worked for. 'It's an NGO that looks after OFWs.' Was all he could manage.

But the operator was a smart cookie, doubtless that's why she had the job. 'We'll send someone right away sir.'

'They've got guns; I think it might be Maa aagh' he managed to yell before he struck a severe blow on the side of the head that sent him sprawling across the floor.

'Get that phone,' yelled the big man. 'Where's that woman? Dam phone!' Turning to her shouted, 'find out who he's been talking to.'

The operator was still on the line and heard the rumpus so she asked the woman for the address.

'Who are you?'

'This is the emergency line; I am calling the police.'

'No, no. No need for the police, everything is ok.'

For her part, the operator thought about it for a few seconds and decided to accede to the request of the police. The police sergeant who took the message contacted his commander who went further up the chain. The words 'Americano kidnapped' was like a red rag.

The police commander called his team together and outlined the problem. 'He was trying to tell us where he was. He said maa...agh.' He directed one officer to find out who is this Rico and Remy Bernardo and this NGO that helped OFW. 'There's lots of NGOs and a million Ricos in Manila,' grumbled the police chief, but find this one,' as he shooed them out of his office to begin the search, holding back his best men. He ordered them to fetch a directory of streets and list on his white board all the names beginning with 'ma'. 'Think about where these streets are,' he said, 'what's the area like?' They discussed all the names like, Mabuhay, Manuael de la Fuente, Malabon, Malate, Magsaysay. 'Magsaysay, that's Tondo there's a lot of crooks there. 'Mabini, that's the tourist area. Mmm, likely. And of course, Old Manila.' He quickly ordered them to search the last three mentioned. 'Each of you, get four men and search these places.'

The officer in charge of the Mabini group declared, 'I think we'll find him there,' so his men enthusiastically began with all buildings on Mabini Street and side streets. At 7.30 that evening the teams assembled in their commander's office. There was not a sign of the Americano despite their house to house searching.

Next morning when they assembled for the day's instructions, they were told there were no changes, but to get out and search. For four days this went on. By this time the press had got hold of the story with garbled accounts of the kidnapping. The police called a press conference and vainly tried to prevent speculation and spelled out the known details but did not mention Joe's work for the

NGO. 'Just call him a tourist, who perhaps had begun to ask too many questions,' said the commander trying to damp down their enthusiasm. But this only fired them up. What sort of questions was he asking? What's behind all this? 'Off you go and tell the people to let us know if they saw anything unusual or suspicious going on with an Americano tourist. Maybe someone saw a drunk looking Americano being taken into a house.

There was a two-story building that was once white, with a steep green roof, fully encased with strong burglar bars over all windows that were blacked out, and the ground floor protected by steel shutters. A couple of patrolling officers stood outside and studied the place. They were new to the area but one said, 'that's a likely place. You can't see in. I wonder what goes on there.'

'No, we've already checked that, besides is all locked up. There's nobody there.'

'But there's no such thing as an empty house in Manila, everyone is full,' argued one of his men.

They were still discussing the place when a decrepit old taxi pulled up, and at that moment, a shutter went up and a door opened and two men raced outside and got into the taxi leaving the door open. It took off in a cloud of exhaust smoke. 'Let's take a look,' said one, drawing his revolver and thumbing back the safety catch. Finger on the trigger he crouched low. They had just entered the door when two more men rushed down the passage knocking them over. The gun fired into the air as the officer landed on his back.

At that moment Joe was recovering from the last stomach blow he had received. Every day two thugs came in and pulled him off the bed and administered two blows to the soil plexus, always leaving him lying on the floor and saying, 'Soon you talk.' But no one ever came to talk with him, by this time a small team of police had arrived and the two officers scrambled outside to report. Quickly sensing what was going on, they began firing at the building. As the bullets came flying into his room, Joe stayed on the floor.

It was a full half hour before the police reached him by which time he was almost paralyzed with fear. Why do they keep firing, he thought? No one is firing back. He was the only one left, the gang had disappeared.

They quickly untied him and demanded a description of his captors. He searched his pockets for a small notebook in which he had noted the number of the taxi and name of the driver. It was missing. All he could remember was that the driver was something like Richard or Ricardo and the taxi number included 626. 'That's probably enough for us to find him,' said the sergeant.

WAITING IN SINGAPORE

As soon as the police had all the information Joe could give them, Remy's people insisted that he leave the country immediately. 'Go to Singapore and wait for me there,' said Ricardo. 'Go to the MIA immediately and we'll send you your luggage and ticket. I'll get my car to take you.' Turning to Remy he said, 'Go and pack up his things and come back here for tickets and hotel vouchers.'

He had five hours to wait for the next available plane to Singapore and he sat on a bench nursing his sore stomach that was a mass of bruises. As far as Joe was concerned meeting people at airports was proving very productive. According to the government department that handled OFW, over 4,000 departing workers passed through Manila International Airport every day and being so friendly, it was easy to engage in conversation with a lonely traveller. Rosa was on her way back to London. He found her drying the last tears after saying goodbye to her family once again. She was off back to London where she was to meet up with her employer. This was her third time away from home after signing a new contract. He was a rather junior Saudi prince whose family benefited from a huge income from oil reserves on their property.

Joe noticed that she was reading an email printout, reading then putting it down breathing out an audible sigh, then taking it up again to read once more. This happened several times until Joe felt that she was becoming anxious about this next job. 'Where are you going?' asked Joe, sitting down beside her. Rather than being left alone with her concerns she readily began to tell him about her work experience overseas.

'My prince,' as she put it, 'is very good to me and so is the princess. She is very sweet. They give me everything I want and much more than I need, but the problem is I never get any rest. But I am willing to sacrifice myself for my family because he sends them all my money all the time. In fact, he hardly gives me any money at all, but sends all my salary back home and we've built a nice family home.'

Rosa explained that as soon as she arrived in Saudi, they opened a bank account for her and got the details of her family's account. The princess said, 'Just tell me what you want and I will give it.'

'This sounds as though you are a very lucky lady.'

'Oh yes I am lucky, but...I don't have any freedom. I am on duty 24/7, no days off, no freedom to do anything. They gave me a nice phone and a computer and pay for everything. I'm just the princess's laundry girl. They have an Indian cook and his wife is a maid and there are two nannies, one for each child. I look after the princess's clothes. There's another girl who does the other laundry. There are others in each of their houses.'

'How many houses?'

'Four I think.'

'Is that bad news?' asked Joe pointing to the paper in her hand.

'It's our travel plans. I go to London and meet the other servants, then we go to Switzerland for a few days then back to Saudi.'

'That sounds ok.'

'Mmm, yes it is, but, I have to wash all her clothes every day and she usually changes at least once a day sometimes twice. Her sleeping clothes have to be washed every day also the bed linen. I've just heard from the Swiss servants and they say that the washing machine and dryer that broke down last time we were there have not yet been repaired or replaced so that makes my job harder.'

'Why don't you tell your boss?'

'I am not allowed to email them or speak to them on the phone: they are very strict about that.'

'Maybe what you can do is text the princess and say, 'Please forgive me for bothering you your highness, but the Swiss servants tell me that the washing machine and dryer have not yet been fixed and because it is so cold there now, it won't be possible to dry the clothes.' I see you have a pretty good phone.'

'Perhaps I can but she won't like it.'

'She won't like wet cold clothes either.'

Another young woman sat down nearby and appeared keen to talk. She was also off to London to join her Saudi employer. Her name was Lisa and had no complaints about her work. However, she had a question about her boss's car. 'Can you tell me about cars,' she asked Joe.

'Well perhaps, what do you want to know?'

'When we go to London my boss always takes me in his car and all the time people stare at us because it is a very strange small car. When you get in, the door opens upwards not sideways. There is always a crowd around us watching. Why would they do that?'

'That sounds like a very special car, possible a Maserati. They are very expensive. Only a very rich man can afford one. Is your boss rich?'

'Yes I think so. He spends money all the time and so does his wife. When she goes shopping, she always goes in a special car and gets a taxi to bring home all her shopping bags. My friend looks after her clothes, that's all she does because the princess never wears the same clothes twice.'

'Are you serious, is she really wearing her clothes only once?'

'Yes sir, nothing is worn twice, underclothes, dresses, everything.'

'What does she do with them?'

'I don't know sir, but there are always boxes of clothes coming and going. I suppose they go to the poor. My friend who looks after her wardrobe told me that there is not just a cupboard for clothes, but a big room like a shop. She hangs up everything for the princess to choose every day. Then at night she throws everything into a basket.'

'Does she ever give you some?'

'Sometimes. Enough for me to send home a parcel every month.'

'Tell me about your boss. Where does he come from?'

'He's Kuwaiti, and he's a prince and he's got two wives. One is very sweet and the other one hates me. But I keep out of her way as she has her own maids. The sweet one has two children and the other one none, so I think that is her problem.'

'What is your job?'

'I'm the prince's personal assistant, not his secretary, that's another girl. I go everywhere with him and do anything for him. He's very strange because he never calls me by my name, instead he calls me Friday. Why would he call me Friday?'

'That's because you are his helper. It comes from an English story of a man called Robinson Crusoe who had someone to help him and he called him his Man Friday. He met him on a Friday and he became very helpful and efficient. Now days you can call a woman a Man Friday. Actually, it is a great compliment to be called that. It shows that you are very helpful and useful.'

CHAPTER THIRTEEN

Escorted by two policemen, Remy found Joe at the airport and handed over his luggage and tickets. He was surprised to find one in Singapore and an open one to Sydney. 'The boss wants you to wait for him in Singapore and then you can have a break for a while. Go and visit family and friends in Australia. Don't go to New Zealand just yet.' She could see he was in pain so asked the policemen to take them to the airport doctor.

'How did this happen,' asked the doctor, a young woman hardly out of medical school, pulling down his shorts and touching his stomach carefully.

'You don't need to ask,' snapped a policeman.

'Well, I do need to ask. Was it blows by an instrument or perhaps even a fist? I need to know how deep this injury is.'

'A fist, five fists actually, no ten, they hit me twice a day for five days,' said Joe.

'I want him to go to the hospital,' she said, after examining his lower abdomen on all sides. 'I suspect some internal injuries.'

'No, can't do that, he's going to Singapore he can do that there.'

'Ok, but he must not travel alone, he must have a medical person with him.'

Without a word, the police captain called a number and explained the situation to his chief who immediately dispatched a police nurse to the airport. With speed and efficiency that surprised Joe, the police nurse arrived within an hour and made all the hospital arrangements before take-off. 'The Singapore police will do everything for us,' she announced.

'Ok but eat and drink very little until you have seen someone there, and no alcohol,' said the doctor, peeling off her rubber gloves. Then turning to the nurse said, 'Apply this salve to the injury. Be gentle though. You can use that room there. He'll need these to kill the pain, handing over a bottle of tablets.'

'Remember, this is not a massage,' joked Joe as the nurse began smearing on the salve. 'Are you a nurse or a policewoman?'

'I'm a police nurse.'

'Are you a police officer?'

'Yes, I trained as a nurse then as a police officer.'

'Will you have a holiday with me in Singapore?' he grinned.

'No, no, I think you are being naughty. I will return here as soon as I have delivered you to the Singapore police medical team. They will meet us at the airport. They are very good, I know, because I did this last month.' There was a plane due to leave, the one that had no room for him, but mysteriously, suddenly there were a couple of seats.

They were good all right. A doctor and a nurse were at the aircraft door with a wheelchair and whisked Joe off to the hospital after walking him straight through the airport formalities.

The police nurse, her arm around his waist, had escorted him the door of the plane and into the wheelchair. After handing the paperwork to the doctor, bent down and kissed Joe on the forehead and whispered, 'sorry to leave you. Good luck.'

A stern-faced Chinese doctor carefully examined Joe

and, after checking the results of the scan, muttered a few Latin words – like 'purple something' and decided that he required five days of bed rest, two in the hospital and three in a good hotel. There is internal bruising but should heal in good time was his opinion.

That's where Remy and Rico found him, sitting up in bed playing with the electric curtains and blinds that he could operate from his four-star hotel bed. 'Would you like to see it?' he said, pulling up his pyjama jacket to display the entire abdomen that was a huge blue-black bruise. Remy fell to her knees weeping and grasping his hand said, "Oh Joe, you did that for my people.'

'Do you feel like talking now,' asked Rico.

'Go ahead, so long as I can lie down, this thing gets a bit sore if I sit up too long.'

'We have located the gang that caught you, thanks to the taxi driver because he is part of it. It's a bit like an octopus though with many legs. You cut one off and there are seven more. However, we have arrested nine people altogether and the woman that you saw, you know, the one who kissed your ear, is singing like a bird. She's been granted immunity if she comes forward with enough information for us to get the lot.

'We have got all their cell phones and SIM cards: they had 37 altogether. Can you believe that? In some cases, they used a SIM card only once or twice to avoid detection. The police are checking all the info that they have in them. One important immigration official's name keeps coming up so he'll be a big catch. There's also a senior passport officer involved and who knows who else. There are hundreds of numbers to check.

'We want you to go to Australia for a break and we'll be in touch as to your next assignment.

'Wait a bit,' said Joe. 'Who said I want another assignment?'

'We have decided to offer you a 2-year contract and residency in the Philippines if you so desire. Here are the papers. Study them overnight and I'll return in the morning to collect them.' With that, he shook his hand and turning to Remy said, 'I'll leave you to look after him for a while.'

Remy sat on his bed and leaning over kissed him. He put his arms around her and said, 'Sorry I can't hold you too tightly. Give me a week.'

By the end of another week the pain had almost gone but the bruising would take a few weeks to clear and he was ready to travel to Sydney.

Remy was in tears. 'I'm going to miss you so much,' holding him tight, 'Please be careful in Australia. We know about some bad people there.'

The plan was that Joe would spend a couple of weeks visiting relatives whom he had not seen for some time. His cousin was glad to put him up and when his wife saw him wince and touch his stomach as he picked up his bag she said, 'What's wrong. You're hurt.'

'I'm all right.'

'No you are not. Come on now, I'm a nurse let me see.'

'Ok you're coming with me to see the doctor.'

'No, no need. I've seen one in Singapore and he's given me stuff to take.'

'Ok then, I'll apply the salve myself. I know about this one, it's got to on every twelve hours and you can't reach around the back where the bruising is still bad.

After He had hardly sat down at the table for the evening meal when his great nephew asked what he had been doing lately. He briefly described his time in Japan and the Middle East when his great niece said, 'you don't have to travel so far to get stories like that. Here in Aussie we have heard of some terrible things of the way some outback people have been treating their foreign workers.

'The people over the back,' said his nephew, waving his arm toward their neighbours, 'have got a farm way out and they have just got back from their annual visit. They are ok, they're good sorts, but their neighbours are the ones you should know about. We can see them tonight if you like.'

'I don't mind meeting them,' said Joe, 'but I can't depend on hearsay. How far away do they live?'

A quick text to Manila soon confirmed that he should check them out. They already had a few stories drifting back from Australia and would be pleased to have some definitive information. 'We know that the government there would put a stop to whatever is going on but we need the facts.'

'Well, you point your car due West and drive for about 16 hours. You'll find them about there.'

But his wife spoke up with 'you're not going anywhere for a week, not with bruising like that.' She stood up and reached for the keys of the rental car that had just been delivered. 'We're sending this back and delay it a week.' His objections were easily overcome so he enjoyed a holiday of reading, resting and eating.

When he finally hit the road, the directions were amazingly accurate for after leaving at 6 am and driving through a few small towns, each glorying their service station, roadside pub and fast-food joints, at exactly 10 pm he arrived at an isolated pub called 'The Stony Creek.' It was a single-story structure with a rusty corrugated iron roof and two old utes that had seen better days parked outside. A barman, who imagined he was still in an inner-city bar with his long-sleeved white shirt and black bow tie, was soon giving directions to the farm (which also advertised home stays) he was looking for. 'You might want to consider staying with us for the night,' he suggested, and with undisguised contempt said, 'we have clean rooms and edible food.'

Joe was the only overnight visitor and the only customer for food and drink. The barman was also the cook and waiter. 'If I get more than six, I call the boss.' This gave him the opportunity of finding out all he could about the Laubanoski farm.

'Are they South Africans or Polish,' asked Joe.

'Why would you want to know that? What are you after? You are not the usual kind of visitor they get. What'ya selling. You're not a shearer that I can tell. Let me tell you, if you are selling get the money first.'

'Tell me about the place, what's it like?'

'What do you want to know. They run sheep, thousands of them. What'd you trying to sell or buy?'

'I'm not selling anything; I just want to meet some of their staff: some of them are friends of mine.'

'Friends! How can they be friends? All they've got are a few abos and some Asians.'

'Asians. That's right, my friends are Asians.'

'You have friends who are Asians! Come on man, they're not Australians, actually, you're not either, are you?

Mmm thought Joe, so this is an example of racism outback-Australian style. Why won't I be surprised at what I will find on the farm?

He found the Laubanoski Farm at the end of a 50-kilometre dusty track through scrubland. The main house was a typical single story unkempt looking place with perished paint and an overgrown garden. To one side was a long building that housed the workers. It was a simple series of about 20 rooms joined together with long veranda standing on foot high foundations. Another derelict looking building stood to one side with an obvious look of a cookhouse.

No sooner had he pulled up at the front door when a large white man clads in a pair shorts and singlet appeared at the front door filling it almost completely and bellowing 'Vat do you want? I vat nothing. No visitors today,' and slammed the door shut.

This is not going to be easy, though Joe. Maybe I'll just wait here for a while and see what happens. Ten minutes later the farmer opened the door and yelled,

'You still here?'

'I have some friends from the Philippines working for you and I'd like to see them.'

'Everybody work, you government?'

'No, no, I'm not the government, just a friend. I'll come back tonight,' and without waiting for a response started the motor.

'Ok tonight. Ok.'

Back at the hotel the barman-cook-waiter was anxious to know how he got on with 'that guy.' 'You'll be lucky to see anyone; he's notorious for keeping a watch over his people. He doesn't like visitors of any kind, you ought to see the way he handles the government fellows. They get a short shrift every time until they learned to take a policeman with them.'

It suddenly occurred to Joe why he thought there was something different or strange about the farm. There were no dogs in evidence. An hour before sundown he set off again. The place was a hive of activity with people walking to and from the cook-house carrying plates of food to their rooms. There appeared to be an equal number of men and women all Asians and, as far as he could tell, all from the Philippines. A tall fellow came over and after politely greeting him asked if he could help. 'I'm the supervisor of these people,' he said, is there something I can do for you?'

'Please have your meal and after that we can have a quiet chat.'

'What do you want to chat about?'

'Please eat first, then I will explain.'

'Tell me now quickly, the boss doesn't like us talking to anyone from outside.'

Joe had to quickly sum up the situation and decided that he had better be up front because this man looked like a responsible type. After all, he was the supervisor. 'I represent an NGO from Manila that is concerned for the welfare of OFWs. I just want to see that everything is ok with you all here, especially the women.'

'The women are ok because we try to look after them. We are all having problems here.'

A few quick questions later Joe discovered that their main problems were to do with excessive working hours, no days off and long delays in their wages being paid. Their contracts meant nothing. No one was allowed away from the farm except for a medical emergency. A mobile shop covered all their needs. Purchases were meticulously recorded and paid by the farmer who deducted them from their wages. At that very moment a loud horn blast signalled the arrival of the mobile shop.

It was an old five-tonne lorry driven by an elderly Greek. His wife, seated beside him, clad in a black headscarf, sold only to the women. The truck was fitted out with shelves of daily necessities like soap, shampoo, towels, cheap garments, toiletries, cheap watches and plastic jewellery. A roughly painted sign above a small cabinet read 'Good watch and jewelries.' The farmer and his wife carried out a small table and the workers lined up to show them what they had bought. These were recorded on a simple card system. All this activity gave Joe a few more minutes to converse with the supervisor, Nathan. 'Please go now else I will be on trouble.'

'Maybe I will come again tonight, quietly, secretly, where do you live?'

'I'm on number one.'

'I'll see you at nine.'

'That's too late we'll all be in bed by then. We get up very early. Come at eight.'

Later that night, Joe parked the car about a kilometer from the house and walked quietly into the yard. He hoped he was right about the dogs. There were none. Nathan had left his door ajar. Calling quietly 'may I come in,' he pushed it open to find the small room packed with people. There were five women sitting cross-legged on the bed and seven men on the floor. They all simultaneously whispered a greeting, all smiles in their delight at seeing him. Nathan explained that he had informed them of Joe's visit and his reason for coming to their farm. Politely and quietly many of them told of their experiences at the farm almost all of them saying the same thing. How they had been duped as a group into signing a contract with the farmer's agent in Manila expecting a generous salary and good working and living conditions. He had come from their province of Bicol and told a great story of life in Australia how they would earn lots of money and because there were no shops they could send nearly all of the money back home. All of their families became very excited about this and encouraged them to take the job.

The work was quite strange to them being unused to

sheep farms in the Philippines. They told how they had to chase the sheep around. It was then that Joe realized why he hadn't seen any dogs. He used people to drive the sheep because farmer Laubanoski had a hatred of dogs. Joe reflected on how he would not be able to get white Australians to chase sheep like that. One of the women spoke up and said, 'he's allergic to dogs.' She explained that when he comes home from the market or a sheep sale he is covered in a rash and she has to apply a lotion all over his body to relieve the itch. That is, instead of the regular massage she gives the couple. She was the maid taking care of the cleaning, laundry and providing the lady of the house with all her womanly requirements like hairdressing, nail care and a frequent body massage. 'She needs me because she has a big problem with her muscles. But she's very kind to me, it's just her husband who won't pay me properly.'

There was no sign of abuse or ill-treatment just unfair working conditions and lax payment of wages. Work started at sunrise and went on until sunset every day of the month except the last Sunday when the Catholic priest came to perform a mass for them. They all had similar reasons for being there, to support families back home and their failure to remit funds on a regular basis was the cause of great anxiety. The postal service was irregular and there certainly were neither Internet service nor cell phones. 'We were better off in the boondocks at home than here,' complained one man, 'I've not talked to my wife or children for six months.'

When they were paid, usually about every second or third month, it took a lot of persuasion to be allowed to remit funds back home. It was the intervention of his wife that corrected this. The farmer thought that because there were no shops, they couldn't spend the money so they didn't need it. When their first pay was made, it was only half the amount indicated in the contract.

He claimed the balance was for their keep even though the contract called for full board and lodgings plus the specified monthly cash payment.

Nathan then produced from a plastic bag hanging on a nail ('this is my filing cabinet' he joked) an envelope that contained a long list of grievances. It clearly stated all the facts and was exactly what Joe needed. Giving it to Joe in a polite Philippine fashion holding it with two hands and slightly bowing said, 'Can you pass this on to the people who should know about us and maybe can help us?'

'I certainly can,' said Joe, 'I know people who can help and I am sure they will act quickly. Meantime, may I encourage you to continue to work well so that you will l have nothing to be ashamed of.' Amid of a chorus of 'yes we will,' 'thank you for coming,' he left them, all smiles for taking an interest in them. There were a few letters for him to post that had been written in the hope that someone would post them in town. They handed them over saying things like, 'for my grandchildren I haven't seen them for so long.' 'For my dear husband. He's in Saudi.' 'This is for my wife; she's had a new baby.' 'For my girlfriend, at least I hope she's still my girlfriend.'

On the way back to Sydney, he stopped at the first town where he could find photocopying and scanning services so that a full record of their grievances could be sent to everyone who needed them. He considered contacting the Australian police but they could do nothing without a formal complaint. The police prosecutor in the first big town he came to was very interested in his story but with a quick read of the documents he could see that it was not formal complaint. 'But don't worry,' he said, 'we'll find a way around this. I see he has written asking for the 'appropriate authorities' to do something. Well, I guess that's us.'

'But couldn't a clever lawyer take the line that the 'authorities' could be construed to be their contractor and all the Philippine government departments and people involved in getting them employment? Believe you me there will be many.'

'Maybe,' but we'll soon find a way of nobbling the bast...d.'

'Shall I tell them to make an official complaint to the police?

'Sure, that might speed things up. Just tell them to write a simple note, a one-line request to us along with a copy of all this stuff and we will get right on to it.' Joe hesitated, 'I'm wondering if old Laubanoski will let me back there again. He's sure to have heard about my clandestine meeting. He won't like that.'

'Tell you what, you write out a simple letter like we need, I'll send a man out with you and you can pass the letter over and get them to sign it. We know this fellow. We'll use an unmarked car so as to not stir things up too soon.'

Joe prepared a list of all the names and addresses of people they would need to know but at the same time was not a little concerned that the end of this could be they all lose their jobs. They might do nothing and be prepared to stick it out and hope for full payment at the end of the contract.

He collected a large basket of fresh fruit and lots of chocolate that drew loud calls of joy from the group that surrounded the car. The farmer appeared very quickly but Joe held up an orange and said, 'I've just brought them some treats from their friends.' He shrugged his shoulders and went back inside. Handing the letter over to Nathan he told him to have the letter signed by the entire group. Call them one by one to your room and sign and give the letter to this man.'

'Who's she?'

'He's a plain-clothes detective. He's going to help you.

He can only do this after you have signed the letter. The law in Australia is on your side so don't worry about anything.'

But it all turned out, as he had feared. At the end of his two-week holiday, he called the detective in Shepperton. Although the group had signed the complaint letter, they so feared their farmer would dismiss them all and send them home and they would end up with nothing, they withdrew the letter and so the police could do nothing. When approached by the police, the farmer had given assurances that by the end of their contracts, he would have had such good sales that he would be able to pay them out fully and send them home with their bank balances bulging.

CHAPTER FOURTEEN

As soon as Joe received his special visa he was off back to Manila. This time he arrived at midday, a really busy time. The border procedure took two hours and both Remy and Renny were there to meet him. Later he reflected on their welcome. They both kissed me twice. Usually, the people here only kiss once unless you are very special. Here I am, with a residence visa and I'm free to marry one of them if I like. It's not quite the same thing as my American friend with his twins!

A special meeting had been arranged with Remy's people plus a number of important government officials. Joe was asked to address them on the question of the philosophy of the OFW programme. The meeting turned out to be a fascinating display of civil servants striving to support government policies but at the same time without admitting it, trying to acknowledge the fact that they faced enormous problems both economic and social.

Many considered President Marcos' idea of encouraging people to work overseas on a contract basis, to be quite brilliant. He believed it would be a boost to the economy of the country as well as the families of the workers. Quite quickly it took on a life of its own increasing steadily until it had reached a significant level of importance on every front. The government people were very quick to explain the official policy toward OFW. They pointed out the Labor Law enacted on May 1974 [4]made careful provisions for both government and people. To begin with, it was considered a stop-gap measure to generate jobs.

There were a number of carefully thought-out provisions to protect the workers but over the years due to corruption and lassitude some enormous problems had arisen. Later in 1995 it declared (R.A. 8042) 'The state does not promote overseas employment as a means to sustain economic growth and achieve national development.'

However, today the overseas employment programme has become 'permanently temporary.'

'There can be no debate on the value of the remittances sent back by OFW,' said Joe. 'The latest figure I have seen amounts to just over US$20 billion sent home last year. And one problem that has occurred is that so much of this money is spent of immediate family needs such as medical expenses, education and paying off debts and so little invested in long term items such as a family home or business. However, the latest report from Bangko Sentral ng Pilipinas (BSP) I indicates that a larger percentage of remittances is now being invested wisely – more than 30%.

'But there are two sides to this problem,' he declared, 'You could easily give a long lecture on the economic benefits that OFW brings to the country and we would all be so pleased with it. But, let the social and spiritual workers make a statement and they will tell of very severe problems emerging.

'There is yet another problem before us, that of people working illegally. In many cases, they put themselves out of reach of the government agencies.

'Our NGO is concerned with the welfare of our people. Look at this piece from the Agence France-Presse on 12/06/12. I've made a copy for you all. Let's pause a moment to read it. Although this a public document I have changed the name of the individual involved.'

'Filipina maids abused, raped by employers in Morocco. RABAT - Young women from the Philippines working as housemaids in Morocco on Wednesday described being exploited, physically abused and raped by their employers in the North African kingdom.

"I was confined in the house of this woman, who confiscated my passport. To get it back, she told me that I had to give her $4,000," Ana Bernardo, a young Filipina, told reporters at a press conference in Rabat.

"I'm ready to give up the job that I've done for two and a half years and return to my country," she said, before shouting, with tears in her eyes: "My employer raped me."

"When I arrived in Morocco, I was hired by a woman who beat me regularly," another woman told the conference, convened by the Democratic Organization of Labour (OTD), weeping as she spoke.

The honorary consul for the Philippines, Porto Joselito, said there are around 3,000 young Filipino housemaids in Morocco.

"Most of them are victims of poor treatment and exploitation, including sexual exploitation," he said.

Marcel Amiyeto, the secretary general of the immigrant workers' section of the ODT, one of Morocco's main trade unions, backed up the claims.

"Some of them have been raped or have been subjected to violence by the women that employ them, others have gone without being paid for more than a year," Amiyeto said.

Social Affairs Minister Bassima Hakkawi was not immediately reachable for comment.

Filipino housemaids in Morocco often have no work contracts and earn less than the minimum wage, of around 240 euros per month.

This highlights the great problem that exists with people working illegally in foreign countries. We are told that there is a great number of illegals from several Asian countries in Saudi Arabia and their recent effort to combat this problem can be seen in the new regulations regarding cell phones.'

'The second paper I have given you describes what the Saudi Government is doing. Let's read it.'

'Undocumented migrants in Saudi Arabia may soon find it difficult to connect with their families in the Philippines following the implementation of Saudi's new SIM card registration policy.

According to the Filipino migrant rights group Migrante-Middle East, Saudi's Communication and Information Technology Commission will implement a new regulation requiring phone users to input their national identification number (Iqama) immediately after entering their prepaid card number to load-up or transfer balances.

'Saudi telecommunication companies said last week failure to do this would cause disconnection of SIM card services.

Migrante regional coordinator John Leonard Monterona said thousands of undocumented migrants who have not updated identification numbers will be affected by the policy.

"It is a common knowledge that there are thousands of undocumented migrants, including Filipinos, in Saudi Arabia," he said. Obviously, the Iqama or identification card of an undocumented is expired, so he or she will not be able to update or register to continue using a SIM card or to get a new one, Monterona added.'

'To keep a balance in this matter, let's remember the good that has been done, and the way so many families have been helped. I have invited a couple of young women to speak to us today and tell their story. I am pleased to introduce Joy Garcia. My first contact with Joy was as a pen pal. Joy was looking for a friend with whom she could discuss her joys and problems. I very quickly discovered that she had a very interesting story to tell.

'Welcome Joy.'

'Thank you, sir, for this opportunity to meet you all today. I've never been an OFW but my mother has. I'm the product of a dedicated mother who has worked very hard for many years so that me and my siblings and their families could have a good education.

'Mother lives and works in Israel where she is the carer of an 80-year-old man. For 8 years she has taken care of his every need. Although he lives with his wife and family my mother's job is taking care of him as his private carer and nurse. His ancient body is quite frail and she needs to massage his feet and hands regularly to keep the blood flowing and apply lotion to his dry skin. There are other helpers in the home to take care of cleaning, laundry and cooking so mother's full time is for him.

After being with him for eight years, he sometimes jokes with his wife that he ought to marry his carer because she takes such good care of him, but his wife just laughs.' Before leaving the Philippines for this job Linda was required to take lessons in Hebrew and has now become quite fluent.

'One of the nice things about this job is that her employer owns a string of restaurants and a swimming resort so Linda gets to have frequent delicious meals and fears she is putting on weight.

'Linda is paid well and is given a day off every week when she can meet up with friends and sometimes go to church. But these days the difficulty of being away from the family is somewhat eased with frequent contacts through Skype usually three times a week.

'Thanks to my mother I am a trained teacher and so I am very grateful to our government that has made it possible for people like my mother to get work that has been so good for our family.'

After lunch, Joe told the meeting that he had just received an email from a young woman whose mother had worked in Hong Kong for many years so that she could receive the best possible education. She herself was visiting to Hong Kong at that moment and wrote I am currently on a vacation leave right now. Guess where I am at? :) Hongkong! :) We went to Ocean Park yesterday and I saw many Filipina as domestic helpers. I feel that I owe each one of them something. It's like I am connected with each one of them. I gave everyone a smile. They all smile back. I wanted to give each of them a hug and say thank you. I can't help but cry. Seeing them carrying bags and kids etc. It's like a trip down memory lane for me. I am going to stay here until Thursday to go to Disney and to Macau. I feel like going back to Manila asap and just thank and hug my mom for everything. I feel so blessed really. I'll keep you posted Mr. Harvey! Thank you for the all the updates in your newsletter.

God bless you.

Much love,

Tessa

'I know a good deal about this young woman,' Joe told the meeting. 'When Tessa was a small baby she became very ill, and her mother took her to the hospital. But because she had no money she was turned away, despite the fact that the child had begun to turn blue. Even her husband who had deserted the family refused to help. After being turned down for a loan from all her family and friends, she finally took her precious wristwatch to a pawnbroker. When she was older and heard this story,

Tessa decided that as soon as she could afford it, she would buy herself the best wristwatch she could afford. This would be a symbol of security for her. 'It will be gold Rolex, encrusted with diamonds,' she said. 'It will not be only an object of security, but a symbol of my mother's love.'

'There is another interesting thing about this young woman. She comes from a family that does not have the best record of family relationships. All eight of her mother's siblings have had broken marriages. Her own father abandoned her as a baby, and her brother's marriage has failed. She has grown up not being able to trust a man. After a checkered career at school she matured, and on graduating with a degree, has done well in her work and is now a vice president of the prestigious finance company.

'But never from her thoughts is the fact that her mother, realizing that the girl needed the best possible education that money could buy, left her in the care of her mother and worked in Hong Kong for 10 years. She told her daughter that she would not come back for any ceremony except the one in which she was the top of the class. This spurred her on to do so well that she achieved this. Attending the best schools meant that her all her classmates became successful and thus she has a good circle of close friends in important positions. This was exactly her mother's dream.

'Her mother, I should add, was first hired by me as my secretary and part-time domestic helper for my wife. When she first applied for the job, I had made it clear that I wanted a single woman, not a mother of small children. My wife and I did not like the idea of taking a mother away from her children. 'I'm single' she assured me, so I hired her and took her to Hong Kong. A few months later, she confessed to being mother of two, but by that time, she had won a place in our hearts and she stayed with us for several years until we were moved from Hong Kong.'

There followed an intense discussion on the right and wrongs of the programme. On the one hand it is of great importance to the economy of the country and the welfare of many of the people. On the other, there is a generation of children growing up not knowing the daily love and care of a mother. The wonderful family spirit so obvious in the Philippines was not always meeting the need of growing young children. It is true than children learn and adapt relatively easily but for many, they grow up with a feeling of loss deep in their hearts.

Joe stood up and called them to order saying, 'let me read this to you. Loung Ung is the Cambodian woman who wrote so intimately about her life as a young child under the dreadful Pol Pot regime said in her book. First, they Killed my Father, "By telling the story through a child's eyes I hoped to dispel the myth that children suffer less than adult in their traumatic experiences. While growing up in Vermont, I used to get so angry when I heard people say to my brother Meng, 'isn't it lucky she was so young when she went through the war. Maybe she won't remember at all. She'll adapt faster and heal faster because she was so young.' Oh, how I wanted to scream out: 'I remembered I saw! I hurt!' But I did not have the words to explain what I felt. When the words came to me, I found I did not have the courage to say them out loud…I wanted my readers to know the confused mind, the lost soul the lonely life and angry heart of the child I was, when my charmed life and family were taken from me by the Khmer Rouge, and I did not understand a single thing that was going on.'

Ricardo then asked the meeting what they should ask Joe and Remy to do. We have to decide their next job. Personally, I think we should send them to Lebanon. There have been many difficulties for our people there and I know that government is becoming very concerned about the situation especially of domestic workers seeing that there are no protecting devices there for them. There was immediate agreement from all present, and Ricardo turned to Joe and said, 'there you are, that's want we want.'

'Lebanon, yes, right, ok. I know a little about the place. It's still recovering from the civil war, but its more or less at peace now.'

Remy and Joe were having dinner at his hotel when there was a text from a woman who had a story to tell. 'I'll call back later,' answered Remy. A few minutes later there was another text – 'Please call me again. I have a story.'

Joe was impressed how quickly this NGO operated. He was handed tickets and visa for Lebanon within 24 hours after agreeing to go there.

At the airport he was surrounded by men and women heading for overseas work. He chatted with a small group of seamen and then to two men who were professional welders on contract to an oil company in Nigeria. Welders were probably the highest paid workers and Joe said, 'you fellows get the best wages.'

'Yes, best wages but worst conditions.'

'Yeah, good pay bad place,' said the other. 'Sorry, can't talk, we have to go now.'

This left a young woman seated nearby who appeared to want to talk.

'Where are you off to?'

'Middle East.'

'First time?'

'Yes.'

'Which country?'

'Bey, beetroot, ah beyroot.'

'Really? So am I.'

'But I'm going to see my sister in Singapore first, then go to that place.'

'Do you know where you will work? Maybe you have the phone number.'

'All I have is my recruitment agency's number,' and held out a card with the number.

'Do you mind if I make a note of it? Maybe I can call you next week.'

'Will you? That would be good.'

'Ok, here's my name but I don't have a Beirut number yet.'

He noticed a man sitting nearby who seemed to be taking an interest in their conversation, so he said, 'so he said, 'Let's talk elsewhere come with me and I'll get us a drink.' Ten minutes later he saw the same fellow sitting right behind him.

Three hours later on the plane to Beirut, he took his customary hourly walk the length of the plane to keep the circulation going. And there several rows back were this same man. No problem with that, after all they had met at the airport.

An embassy official was on the airplane's steps to meet him. The plane had been parked a bus ride from the terminal, and as one passenger remarked as they boarded the bus, trust our airline to park here. Not so expensive. They had no sooner entered the terminal door when a quiet voice in his ear said, Mr. Joe. I'm Melanie.' She was a young woman from the embassy. "Don't worry sir, we always meet our visitors here. Give me your passport and papers." She whisked him around the customs desks and to a VIP immigration counter. The place was in turmoil with three Jumbos disgorging their passengers all at the same time.

A dark blue Mercedes drew up beside them with Melanie urging him to get in quickly and leave the luggage for the porter to load. 'This place has changed. Last time I was here it was at the end of the civil war and everything was in ruins. You know Melanie my first time here was in the seventies and Beirut was called the Paris of the east. Everything was duty-free, good food, accommodation was cheap. We stayed at the Bristol hotel. It was beautiful, old world, no chromium plated fittings but highly polished wood. The kids were too young to eat in the dining room so they had a hotel maid feed them in the room.'

'We've still got maids here and luxury hotels, but we want you to be careful where you go and who you talk to. I'll pick you up in the morning at 10. There will be a meeting with the ambassador and our security people at 10.30.'

Joe felt like taking a long walk but decided against it, took a hot bath and retired.

The hotel was French run so breakfast was really good coffee and croissants. The waitress was a Filipina, and he was soon asked about her time in Lebanon. 'There are many of us here sir and...' a quiet cough behind her sent her scuttling away. It was the "maître ' d".

'Sorry sir if she is bothering you.'

'No not at all, she was answering my question.'

'Do you have many foreigners on your staff?'

'Sorry sir, but I find that a strange question. Lebanon is multicultural and always has been' and walked away.

The embassy car was right on time and as Melanie ushered him inside said, we must hurry the meeting has been brought forward to start as soon as you arrive.

The ambassador's smile of welcome did not quite hide

his concern about Joe's visit. He began the meeting expressing doubts about Joe's intentions, but shrugging his shoulders, agreed to cooperate as much as possible: he'd had his instructions from Manila. A military attaché and another soldier-looking type were present at the meeting.

After the brief but guarded welcome Joe began to describe the work of the NGO but the ambassador quickly spoke up and said, 'We know all about it. Just be careful. I have called your off-sider to come as I think she's needed here. She's due here tomorrow. Meantime, please allow Melanie to show you around the town,' and turning to her, he said, 'Give him a good Beirut lunch and look after him all day.'

This city has its quota of great restaurants and Joe suggested they find a nice quiet place where they could talk. He soon found out that Melanie had done her homework and was full of suggestions as to who he could meet. One of her duties was to keep in touch with Philippine citizens living in the country. In her three years in Beirut, she had met Filipinas who were having difficulties with their employers. Most of them had good jobs and were very happy but there were always a few who had been unlucky.

After lunch she advised Joe to return to the hotel and rest and then she and her husband would take him out to dinner at a restaurant high in the nearby mountains. As they gazed out over the scene of the city below and deep blue Mediterranean that reached to the horizon Joe remarked, 'I can't see any sign of burning buildings or puffs of smoke from mortars. No rattle of machine guns. The place is at peace at last.'

That called for him to describe the place when he was there during the civil war. One day a street would be blocked by rebels, the next day it would be open and the one nearby was controlled by another armed group. You've no idea how complicated the civil war was, he told them.

'It took a long time for a foreigner to understand who was fighting who, as there were at least seventeen different groups plus a variety of pro-Palestinian organizations. 'One photojournalist described Beirut as 'a place where you could never figure out who was killing who or why.' I was arrested five times, three times in my first two days here. Block after block had been destroyed; it truly was a war zone.

'I was staying with a family who had two Filipinas helping in their large home. I remember them saying, we love it here so long as we stay inside! Rockets hit houses on both sides but not their place and the only problem they had was sweeping up all the dust they create! Brave women. They said, "Our family is here to serve God and that's what we do." As far as Filipinos were concerned, in those days they were a rarity. But in recent years their number had grown to over 30,000. The problem was that it was an easy country to enter, and many did not have legal contracts. Thus, they became the target of some illegal manpower companies and recruitment agencies.

Remy arrived next day and was a little surprised to find that she was declared to be Joe's partner, not in only work, but domestically. Joe had been out sightseeing with the military attaché and on returning to his hotel, found Remy settled into their luxurious two-bedroom suite.

They went out for dinner at a nearby restaurant when Joe noticed one of the diners was on his plane. He was easily recognized by his unruly hair that looked as if he hadn't touched it being at Manila airport. Joe put this out of his mind when the man did not seem to notice him even when he deliberately walked near his table on his way to the rest room. Remy had already discovered that there were five Filipina workers at their hotel. They were housed in a nearby apartment. 'We'll go there tonight and meet the day shift workers and see where that leads us,' she said. The two whom they met seemed very happy with their work although they didn't like their boss very much. The French maître 'd expected too much of them, they declared. He was constantly suspicious of them. He thinks we are all thieves and wanton women, and they giggled at the thought.

The hotel staff was accommodated in a block of flats opposite the hotel. Speaking Tagalog, Remy explained their mission and they soon provided details of women whom they knew who were having trouble with their employers. They explained that they were all Catholics and met regularly at the church not just on Sundays but often during the week because the church hall is available to them at any time for social gatherings or place where they can have some peace and quiet. However, they warned that so many of them never get any time off, not even a few hours. The only way to meet them was in a secret visit when there was no one at home.

Joe was so thankful that Remy had been sent. When he left Manila there was a half-hearted statement made that they might send her.

Their hotel contacts gave them about twenty numbers to call. Next morning Remy began to systematically ring all the numbers given. The first call was answered by the Lebanese employer. Her response was savage. 'I have told that girl never to tell people our number. No, you can't speak to her.'

'Oh dear,' exclaimed Remy, 'now we have got her into trouble.'

The second one was a little better with the employer giving her maid's mobile number, but saying sternly, 'don't call before ten.'

'When is her day off?' asked Remy.

'Day off! What are you talking about? She's my maid, my maid.'

"Well,' said Joe, 'that tells us she works every day until 10 pm.'

The fourth call was better. Remy was told she could visit her anytime between 9 am and 6 pm when she was alone in the apartment. They immediately went out on the street to hail a taxi. An old brown Mercedes Benz pulled up and Joe gave him the address written on hotel notepaper. 'Ok, ok, wee, wee,' said the driver, then as he drove off called back to them in the rear seat, 'Dis one exclusive ok?' By that Joe knew that he meant he would not stop for other passengers.

It took forty minutes to find the apartment block and the driver said, 'I think it is better to pay a dollar. OK?' Excited at getting a contact so soon, Joe forgot to bargain and handed over a US$20 bill.

They knocked on the door of No 5b and it was opened immediately by a young woman of about 20 but who held her fingers to her mouth saying shshsh. Once inside she said, 'No one must know you are here. I will play music.'

Her story was very sad. On turning 18, Jocelyn's parents allowed her to apply for an overseas position in the hope that it would relieve the family's serious financial situation. A recruiter had come to her village in the province offering a very good job. All the family had to do was pay him the equivalent of US$1,000 and he would get her a job that would pay off the loan and she would soon be sending $500 home every month. Strenuous efforts by the family realized the thousand dollars and within two months a package arrived with her passport and travel documents. It was all so easy and quick.

Politely Jocelyn knelt on the floor before them and told her story. 'Sometimes I feel as though I am going crazy. I work all the time. They go out all day and I am left to work and work. All their family and friends bring their laundry here and I have to wash and iron it. If I don't do it properly or on time or if it gets mixed up, they hit me. She pulls my hair and swings me around. You can see I have long hair and I have never cut it. She has a stick and beats me to it. Look at me,' and she pulled up her top and turning around showed her back that was covered in bruises and scratch marks. 'She's so much bigger than me so I can't fight her back.' Then she turned around, and very unfilipina-like, pulled up her bra to show bruises all over her breasts.

'I am all the time hungry because they don't feed me properly. I can't even eat their leftovers, so I carefully wrap them up and put them in the garbage, and later get them and eat them. Often she asks me to massage them both her and her husband. I can't do that properly and they scream at me if it's too hard or too soft. The husband never speaks to me, doesn't even look at me.'

She has no contract and her employer keeps her passport. They give her a little money and say they are sending the rest of her pay back home but she isn't sure because she can't call her family. The phone is locked. They take her shopping for necessities once a month and they pay for everything.

Remy carefully recorded all the details of the employer and with Joe's knowledge of French was able to find out where the couple worked. In a drawer he found six passports, three for each of them, Lebanese, Syrian and Iraqi, but there was no sign of Jocelyn's.

The maid next door, who gets a day off every month, was the one who told the hotel women about Jocelyn. Remy knocked on her door and was astounded at the difference between the two households. Estella was well cared for by employers who had not just employed her as a nanny to their two small children, but who after five years had grown to love and appreciate her. When she first took up employment with them, the lady of the house explained that if she worked well and that the children grew to love her, then they would regard her not just as a nanny, but as an aunty to the children. She would live with them like a sister. Later she discovered that her employer had a little Philippine blood as her great grand-father was a seaman who had fathered a child to her great-grandmother who was stewardess on his ship. There was no way they could marry but the man who became her husband, quietly married her across the border in Syria. When this was explained to Estella, she said, 'I have always thought you had our eyes.'

There were many calls to make with most of them not being answered. Of the seven that were, five gave very positive responses to their employment situations, but the two negatives were heart breaking. Both had been sexually abused by the man of the house, and in one case, had been offered to his brother. However, there was no problem with salary payments, both were well paid, always on time, but at an awful cost. When they met one girl in a café she confessed to what she called 'an enormous problem.' My employer is very sweet and kind to me, always very gentle and sometimes I like it, but it's wrong, so wrong. What am I to do?'

'You had better see a priest I think, then consider changing your job,' advised Remy. Because there were no contracts involved, changing jobs was easy but the system left the young women vulnerable to unfair exploitation.

Next morning Remy rang nine numbers before getting a reply. Adelita Tengco was a little unsure about meeting them. 'Do you really want to hear my story? I can make it easy for you because I have kept a blog so if you come here, bring a flash drive and you can have a copy. It's in Cebuano, can you read it?'

'No problem,' said Remy.

It was a large four-bedroom apartment not far from the hotel and was in immaculate condition. Adelita kissed them both at the front door exclaiming, 'You are my first visitors ever. I'm not allowed any. Actually, I am very lucky because they don't know I have a notebook computer. I always kept it hidden from them and never let the children see it.' Joe produced a flash drive and Adelita went to her bedroom to make a copy. 'If everything is on here, we won't stay,' said Remy.

'Yes, that's good. They might come back at any time because they are out shopping.' This is my number, use that next time. They returned to the hotel and read her blog. She had for the first up to prepare breakfast for everyone then feed the children and get them ready for school, take them to the front door of the apartment, put them in the car, return immediately without speaking to anyone, except to greet another maid, but no conversation allowed, that's wasting time. The mother always stayed in bed until after the children had gone and didn't even kiss them goodbye.

It hurts me every day to think that their mother never sees them in the morning, no kiss goodbye, they are so small, only 5 and 6 years old. Then I clean up after breakfast, make the beds, wash all the floors, do the laundry then the ironing. One of my duties is to teach the children so I read to them after school. That's always nice to do. Then prepare the evening meal, feed the children, serve the meal to my employers, bathe the children and put them to bed, clean the kitchen and be in bed at 10 o'clock.

I can't communicate with anyone because they lock their phone and took away my own cell phone. So I asked the maid next door to get me another one for ten dollars. Sometimes we could talk to each other very quietly from our windows. She got me another phone and told me she would give it to me the next morning when I put the children in the car. But my employer must have heard us because as soon as I came back, she stood in front of me and held out her hand saying, 'Give me that phone.'

'So we had to do that again and this time they didn't know. After a few months I became very tired, as I never got a day off. I was taken shopping about once a month when I had to buy everything for the family, food, clothes for the children and things for the kitchen. The Madam came with me and handled the money but she wouldn't even let me speak to another maid or anyone else. All I could do was mutter a few words in our language to someone.

'There was one good thing though; they did pay me properly according to the contract so I was able to save nearly all of my money. But I couldn't get to the bank to send any home. It was so frustrating as the family were crying out for help. But there was one big problem for me. My employer kept bugging me and I suppose you can say he was harassing me all the time. At night he would come into my room and I couldn't keep him out because there was no lock on my door. He would beg me to have sex with him. Of course, I refused, besides, I am married with my own children. The first time he came, and I had been there only three days, he asked me very nicely. He told me that he thought that I was very beautiful. I thanked him for the compliment but strongly refused him so he didn't ask a second time. Next night he came again. Same thing. Two nights later, I could see he had been drinking and he became very aggressive. He took hold of my arms and tried to push me on the bed. You can see I am strong. I used to learn karate and a little boxing at high school. My parents were so ashamed of me for doing those violent things. So, when he began to push me, I kneed him in the groin and pushed him hard. He fell to the floor groaning. When he tried to stand up and he was still unbalanced I pushed him out the door. Then I wedged my chair against the door. I could hear him moaning and then after a few minutes he went away.

Next morning when he saw me and his wife wasn't

around, he shook his head and said, 'Tonight I see you, ok?' I said, 'Don't you try.' But he did. He came very late when everyone was asleep and I woke up to find him standing beside my bed. I am much bigger than him. As you can see, I'm no little 45kg Filipina, I'm 70kg. He's a little man. I think he is severely browbeaten by his wife, and in some ways, I feel sorry for him. Fortunately, I had proper pyjamas on, when it is really hot, I wear nothing, so I sprang out of bed and gently pushed him out of the room. He was pleading, 'Don't, please, I am nice man, don't hit.'

After many nights like this, I was able to phone the embassy and they sent someone to rescue me. I just told them that I had to leave because I worked all day and they gave me no time off at all. It was truly difficult because I had come to love the children. A boy of seven and a girl of six. Both beautifully natured and quite unlike their mother. I said nothing about the man, because although he was naughty, he was to be pitied with a wife like that. I had to make my complaint to the embassy staff who came to get me in front of my employer. His wife wasn't there. He gave me a grateful look when he realized I wasn't mentioning him. The embassy arranged for me to take another job for a couple of years before I go home.

They set off to visit another contact they had been given when their taxi was stopped in a back street. A man stood in the middle of the narrow street and stopped the car. Four men appeared and each one opened a door and pulled out Remy and Joe. They slammed the doors and ordered the driver to move off. He began to protest but one pulled a gun and shouted, 'Move or this is for your tyres.' That's a bit stupid thought Joe, how can he move off with punctured tires. Remy was held by a short wiry looking fellow who had no difficulty holding her arms behind her. Joe's assailant was a heavy thickset rogue who pinned his arms down holding him by the wrists with only one hand. Someone kicked at the car doors yelling, 'go, go.'

They were then hustled through the door of an adjacent building, the door slammed shut behind them.

An hour later, heavily blindfolded with stinking black cloths, they were put into a car and taken to another place in the city. As they were pushed into a basement room, they both received a heavy clout on the head that rendered them unconscious for several minutes. Joe regained consciousness to hear Remy quietly sobbing above him. He found himself on the floor under a bed where Remy lay. His hands were tightly bound together with wire.

'What's happening Joe?' Remy whimpered. At that moment the door opened and two men seized Remy saying, 'we don't want you,' and dragged her out, slamming the door behind them. They put her into a car and an hour later, stripped off her blindfold and undid her arms, and pushed her out onto the street, and sped off. Dazed and blinded by the sun, she became aware of a woman's voice saying, 'What's wrong? You all right?'

'Please get me a taxi, I need to go to the Philippine embassy.'

'Where's that?'

'The taxi will know. It's off Independence Avenue.' It was five minutes before closing time and the security guard was not happy about Remy wanting to go in. They had taken her purse, so she had no ID. 'Please let me in, I must see the ambassador, one of our people has been kidnapped. Me too but they let me go. Look at my wrists,' her voice rising in her anxiety. Another guard came to the door and recognizing her, beckoned her inside.

'Please pay the taxi, they've taken my money.'

'That's what they all say,' said the first guard, but his colleague snarled at him saying, 'Tell him to come back later.'

It took half an hour for a meeting of suitable people to be called when Remy poured out her story. The ambassador was very upset bemoaning the fact that he knew their exploits would end like this. 'Tell Manila,' he ordered his aide, 'and let the local people know. His secretary led her away to a small side room where there was a comfortable couch, brought her a drink and encouraged her to rest for a while. Two hours later she was called to a meeting of security people when they pumped her with questions about her experience. When she was being brought into the meeting a uniformed officer was practically yelling at the ambassador shouting, 'Kidnapping is not new here. But this one is not so serious; we call it a commercial kidnap. Mostly we get sectarian ones here like some Muslim group taking a Christian. The ramify, the ramify, the ramific.shons...'

'You mean ramifications, like the consequences,' helped an aide.

'Yes, yes. This sort of thing doesn't start civil wars. It's only about money.'

The ambassador and his team were beginning to look decidedly unhappy. 'This is a serious case for us.'

'Yes, yes, it's serious but to us not serious serious. Mr. Ambassador, leave it to us. We can assure you that we will do our best to locate your man.'

'He's actually our man,' spoke up the representative of the New Zealand Embassy. 'He was working for a Philippine NGO but is one of our citizens. I've received a call from Tel Aviv, and they are offering their help because they have had similar problems with a Philippine gang there. They can send a couple of people over to help.'

'Thanks, but no thanks. We know this work, best leave it with us. Anyway, they should have contacted us first.'

'They did but you refused to speak with them.'

The senior diplomat spoke up, 'Let's leave this in your hands. I'm sure you will do your best,' and rising to his feet signaled the meeting was closed.

'Thank you your Excellency, we will now withdraw and set up our plan of action.'

After the Lebanese team left the New Zealand diplomat explained that a Mossad agent had helped them deal with a gang from the Philippines who were causing trouble with a large group of workers engaged in a building reconstruction programme in which they had brought in over two hundred workers from Manila. They had contracted a team of builders, cooks, housekeepers and medical people, but they discovered that the recruitment agency was operating illegally and thus had produced many unsatisfactory contracts. The Mossad agents had uncovered the problems that led to the prosecution of the gang. As soon as they had dispatched the workers, they disappeared from sight in Manila only to reappear in Kuwait where they hounded the workers for reimbursement of their hiring fees and transport. That's where they caught them.

The New Zealanders contacted Tel Aviv and requested their private and secret assistance to find Joe.

Back at the hotel Remy curled up on the bed whimpering to herself. Suddenly she remembered Joe's New Zealand police friend. He'd left his SIM card from the States in an envelope in the drawer. She quickly fitted it into her phone and ran through the contacts. There it was, at least it looked like the right one beginning with 64. She checked the number in the room phone book. Yes. New Zealand. That's him. He answered her call immediately then had to explain that although they are Interpol and that means international we can't cross borders without following the accepted protocol. But she was not to worry, he would call his Mossad friend unofficially. Within fifteen minutes he called back to say that the Israelis already have people there in Beirut and had been notified and were looking into it, albeit, quietly to begin with.

It was hours since she had last eaten so called room service for a quick meal. There was a quiet knock on the door. 'Who is it,' Remy called standing close to the door and peering through the spy hole. She could see two men. They didn't look like room service.

'Can we come in for a talk. We're from your New Zealand friend.' Cautiously opening the door, she stepped aside and beckoned them in. 'We are from Tel Aviv, but we live here now. We've been ordered to help you find your man. We have asked around and found that this is no commercial thing. No one is asking for money. All they want is for you to stop what you've been doing and get out of here. You go first then they'll send your friend later.'

'But I'm not going without Joe.'

'Once we tell your people they will send you out.'

The older one said, 'Let's sit down and talk about this. You heard what the policeman said, no Israelites, we can do this. Well, they can't. They have still not done anything. Their people are running around asking questions and driving them deeper. We have people here all over. They have found Joe. They know exactly where he is.'

'Is he all right? Where is he? Can we get him?'

'Steady now. You don't know this business. Just stay calm and out of this and leave it to us. We have to see your ambassador and explain the situation to him. He will tell you what to do. He's got to be careful because if he upsets the locals they are not going to be happy about us.'

'But why can't you tell them what you know?'

'Cooperation is a word that's not in their dictionary, not even in French or Arabic! We hope your man is a good diplomat.'

'Let me speak to him first,' said Remy as she stood up to go to the phone. It was ten minutes before they put her through to him and that was only after she assured them that she had very important news about the kidnapping. A secretary insisted she tell her what sort of news but finally relented when Remy threatened to describe her heritage in detail. I have to see him personally and privately as soon as possible. Finally, she was told to come immediately.

But getting her Israeli friends through the front door was the first obstacle. 'Stay here,' she said, 'and I will call for you.'

'Well, what is it?' He said in not a too gentle voice.'

'I have to start at the beginning, sir, so that you will understand.'

'That's a good place to start.'

Speaking in their own language she told him about the NZ Interpol friend and what he had done, 'unofficially and behind his back' she confessed. 'They are outside now waiting to see you sir.'

After a few terse commands to an aide the men were brought in and began a helpful discussion as to how to obtain Joe's release. Right at that moment a call came through from Manila when the real nature of the kidnappers was explained, confirming everything the Israelites had said.

'We can't simply send these men to release him, it's got to be done officially so that we can get the culprits and uncover their operation. Its Lebanese law they have broken not ours.

'Leave this to me. I will talk to the New Zealand ambassador and the local security people and we'll sort something out. You can go now and be assured Joe will be free soon.'

Later that day three sullen security men met with the two ambassadors whose first job was to explain how the Israelites became involved and enforce the notion that there was no official contact made. It was all completely outside their control or knowledge.

'They are clever, they are here and we resent them.

'Our minister is going to be furious,' was their simple response.

'Be glad that they are not causing an international incident but simply helping out on the side,' said the New Zealander. 'Be glad too that the media haven't latched onto this story, yet. We congratulate your staff in this regard. If the story about the reason for your team being here got out, it would look bad for the locals.'

'Yeah, embarrassing whatever way you look at it. However, in one sense we'd like to see this problem aired here. Too many of our people are not being cared for properly. Problem is, it's looking as though it might be our own people behind this.'

'Give it to the media and they will promote the dramatic and avoid mentioning the real problem. I'll get my press officer to write something. The fact is that the Lebanese government has done little to protect contract workers. I know that they have a massive job rebuilding after the civil war. How many buildings were destroyed, hundreds and hundreds. The numbers of foreign workers continue to increase. There are about four times as many Sri Lankan domestic workers here as well as a growing number of Ethiopians. Don't even go there and discuss the treatment some of them get. Another great problem is that many of our people are unregistered, that have no contracts. They just let them in. Our government is wrestling with this problem, however it's not for us to deal with it now. We've got to find a way of getting Joe out,' said the security chief.

It was so obvious that he didn't want to have anything to do with the Israelis when he sighed heavily, coughed loudly, stood up and walked the length of the room a couple of times. Ok I'll send a man to talk to them. But I want him taken alive and shipped out of the country immediately. His girlfriend can go now.'

'She's not his girlfriend, she one of ours, on a dip' passport,' said the Philippine ambassador.

'Never mind, she'd better go.'

'I'm sure our man will be pleased to go,' said the New Zealander.

'But I want the culprits brought to justice. Your minister will support us in this. Have Mr. Joe give us all the evidence we need before he goes. According to our sources, the family who is holding him is not linked to a gang. They seemed to be simply forced to work for one.' He stood up, that's all we can do now. It's over to your people to bring him in and of course track down the main gang who've been breaking your law.'

Ben Solomone the Israeli agent called his team of four together. They discussed the address where they heard Joe was being held. It was an ordinary looking Beirut apartment block with the usual balcony. Directly opposite was another block, almost identical, and unbelievably, the apartment opposite was for rent. Two agents, posing as man and wife, already equipped with fake papers, soon secured a lease and moved in. They hired an Ethiopian maid whom they found on the street, almost destitute and without papers. She gladly took to cleaning out the apartment and set up a small dining table on the balcony.

They set up their usual eavesdropping devices that enabled them to hear conversations of the family opposite. At 22C there was no air conditioning working, and all the windows were open. The first voice was a girl's, 'he's reading the dictionary like a book.' Laughter. 'Hope he can follow the story.' Laughter. Then a man's voice, 'Why don›t you find him a book?' There followed a long discussion in Tagalog.

'We'll have to get a Filipina to help us, contact the boss, he'll know someone.'

'Why not get the girl, whatsaname, er, Remy.'

'OK get her. Buy her a maid's uniform. Make sure she looks the part.'

They brought Remy to the apartment after dark and showed her how the equipment worked. 'Translate and write down everything they say. Keep back from the window and balcony when you've got the earphones on, otherwise its ok if they can see you working. You don't have to wear these all the time. We'll put the speakers on so that we can all hear everything; you just listen out for the Tagalog. Don't worry about the woman speaking French we can handle that.' Now and again, she could detect Joe's voice when the door of his room was left open when they brought him food and emptied his bucket.

    The Mossad agents would not meet the Lebanese security people but insisted on phone contact only. Again and again, they argued as to who would effect the release. The Israelis said they could do it quickly and very quietly. The Lebanese objected saying it was their country, their job, and insisted on being told where to find him. But the Israelis said that they had information about an anti-government group that Lebanon would be pleased to have. Finally, the Beirut people gave in on the assurance that the release was done so quietly that not even the neighbors would not know about it.

Next night at 1 am, the Israeli team assembled and dressed from top to toe in black, entered the building. The security guard was dozing in his chair and fell silently to the floor after a pad of chloroform was held against his face for a few seconds. Three men and a woman silently crept up the stairs to the fourth floor. A specialized Jimmy bar wielded by a muscular agent easily bent the steel frame.

He soon had the steel door open then the main door with its three locks yielded quickly. The plan was to go directly to the room where Joe was being held, while the woman agent was to keep a watch out for family members who might be awake and silence them with the chloroform if necessary.

The Jimmy bar made short work of Joe's door. He was snoring lightly and the agent with the steel cutters had his chain off without even waking him. The chloroform was used again, and the heaviest agent hoisted Joe onto his back in a firemen's hold. Leaving the doors open they were down to the street level in a total of five minutes. The driver moved away quietly and no one in the vicinity was any the wiser. Remy was texted and was down on the street and into the vehicle. One of the agents said, 'We'll leave it to you to explain what happened. He's going to be a bit mystified as to where he is when he wakes up.'

Later that morning, after they had cleared out the flat and left a good donation for the Ethiopian, an agent called the security chief and said only, 'This is the address, we've got him. You'll need French, English and Tagalog to get the full story from the family,' and hung up.

After removing his outer clothing, they put him to bed, Remy sitting beside him watching closely. It was three hours before he woke up to the marvelous sensation of a warm hand gently wiping his brow. 'You're ok now Joe, we got you out of there. Just rest for a while and sleep a little more.

CHAPTER FIFTEEN

On their return to Manila the NGO leadership debriefed the team then called a meeting of appropriate government officials. They explained that the government is continually assessing the situation in all countries where we send workers. Wars come and go, unrest among religious groups, failure of local governments to provide adequate security measures and labour laws that protect our people. There are currently several countries where we have blocked OFW going. They are Afghanistan, Chad, Cuba, Democratic People's Republic of Korea, North Korea, Eritrea, Haiti, Mali, Mauritania, Nepal, Niger, Palestine, Somalia, Uzbekistan, and Zimbabwe.

"As a result of your work, the government has decided to put Lebanon on the blacklist. We will no longer allow our people to go there. That makes fifteen countries on the list. There's a few more that should be on it too. But for now, we want you to take a few days leave.

Later that day, Joe called Ricardo and asked him to meet him for dinner as he wanted to discuss something with him. 'I told you to take some rest.'

'This is not about work, something quite different.'

'Ok, can I bring my wife?'

Joe quickly thought, no way, this is a private matter, then immediately thought, this is the Philippines there aren't so many secrets here, and families get involved in everything. But Ricardo is not family but maybe he's a friend. He's the only male I know here. So he answered, 'Yes, that would be fine.'

Ricardo's wife, Joanne, was lovely and Joe immediately

sensed that she was a good woman who'd understand not just him but Remy too. He was surprised how much she knew about them and could see what was coming. The normally eloquent Joe had difficulty in explaining himself and his feelings for Remy. Joanne reached across the table and took Joe's hand. 'I think we understand perfectly. You've fallen in love and there's only one thing to do. Marry her.'

'You think so? Can I?'

'Of course, you can. There's a well-formed procedure established here. We can help you. I've got a friend who knows all the pitfalls.'

'Pitfalls! Are there pitfalls?'

Ricardo leaned back in his chair and grinned at Joe. Gesturing to his wife he said, 'Just leave it to her. She'll see you right.'

'Wait a bit, I haven't asked her yet.'

"Sure. We'll wait and expect a phone call by tomorrow night,' smiled Joanne. 'If she says no, then I've got some friends who would make wonderful candidates.'

'Please don't get me wrong, I never came here looking for a wife. It's only four months since my wife died and I'm a bit embarrassed to be talking like this so soon. It's just that Remy would be so good for me.

'If she's fallen in love with you, she'll wait. Don't worry.'

That night Joe tossed and turned unable to sleep. What to do about Remy? He thought back to the days when he tried to decide whether to marry his wife. What was it really like to fall in love? One student friend perhaps sensing that he was unable to make up his mind about his girlfriend, gave him a booklet entitled 'How to Know if you've Fallen in Love.' It asked questions like 'Can you not stop thinking about her?' and 'What will your life be like without her?' What will my family and friends think? Too bad what they think, I'm the one to be happy not them! He began to quietly pray about it. That must have settled him down as he went to sleep still praying. He woke at dawn, his mind at peace, and his heart full of joy. Why do I feel so happy? he thought. I know, its because I want to marry Remy. The more he thought about it, the happier he became.

They met up at Ricardo's office next morning and as saw as he saw her he was smitten. She's never looked so attractive as she does now. His joy at seeing her was so obvious she responded with a look that was nothing less than sheer love. He took her hand and squeezed it in such a way she glanced up with a look that said 'It feels like that you have fallen in love with me.'

Rico talked with them all morning about the assignments they were considering. Joe tried to concentrate but by lunchtime Ric sensed that Joe's mind was not on the subject, so he said, 'Take the rest of the day off, you two need to have a long talk.' How does he know that thought Joe: is it so obvious that I've fall in love?

'Let's buy some lunch over the road at the Chowking Restaurant and find a nice shady tree in Rizal Park where we can have a nice long talk,' he suggested. After they had eaten he said, 'Do you know why he has given us the rest of the day off? It's because he can see that I have fallen in love with you, and he's right. We need to talk.' Without further ado he said, 'Remy will you marry me?'

Her response was immediate and leaning over kissed him passionately. 'I guess that's your answer. I am so happy but there are a lot of things that we need to talk about before we go any further.'

The discussed the fact that they both knew of many mixed marriages, how some of them were very successful and others ended in disaster. The foundation had to be true love and cultural differences must be understood and accepted. There were many things to agree on like religion, citizenship, what if there were children, where would they live, does he have to become a Filipino or she a Westerner either Canadian or New Zealander.

'Well you know I like American culture and what I know of you I like. But there will be no children, I can't have them. I had a miscarriage that went wrong, so I suppose you will want to rethink your proposal.'

'Not at all. That's no problem. I've got kids but I am sorry for you though.

'Next question is when. She has to give ten days notice to the registrar,' said Joe.

'Ten days! Ten days, are you mad? It will take longer than that to arrange everything,' said Remy. 'Oh just a minute, yes I think you are right. Let's do it quickly. I don't want to wait either. We can have a simple do at my mother's place. My father told me that a daughter should have one decent wedding with all the trimmings and if there is a second one, it should be a simple affair. I've had one. But there are a few rules we have to observe. Let's ask Joanne to help us.'

Joanne was delighted to receive them. Grinning from ear to ear she sat them down in her sala and explained some procedures they have to follow. There were social courses required for women going overseas to marry a foreigner. 'That won't work,' said Joe, 'I'm the foreigner and I'm here and not overseas.

'There are other regulations that involve you. Just leave it to me and I'll sort it out for you. Tell me, when do you want to marry?'

'Joe wants as soon as possible; he says ten days.'

'OK I'll see what I can do. But I think that may be a bit

soon. There are so many of our people who marry foreigners that there's host of regulations to cover all cases. There's a government department called Pre-Departure Orientation Seminar (PDOS). The PDOS is aimed to prepare Filipinos for the realities of cross-cultural marriages. That is the Commission on Filipino Overseas Migrant and Integration and Education Division. I know about this as I've helped other people. Do you want a church or civil ceremony?'

'We are both Christians but a civil one will be all right. I think that's faster,' said Remy.

'True. They will want counselling courses and family planning and all that. Leave it to me.'

'You might want these,' said Joe, handing over a large envelope containing several copies of his passport, birth certificate, marriage certificate and death certificate of his wife.'

'I'm impressed,' said Joanne, 'Looks like I understand a few things about government. These things take time but one item you must have before we can d much is to obtain something from your embassy before you can apply for a marriage licence. It's called a "Legal Capacity to Contract Marriage." We have a lawyer friend, actually she's my cousin, and she will put you on the right track quickly as it is possible. As soon as they stood up to go after taking a merianda, Joanne hugged them both whispering in whispering in their ears, 'I am so happy. This is good.'

Next stop is your mom's place, what is she going to say about this?'

'She's going to be very happy. She's already told me to marry you.'

'Is that true?'

'What she said was, 'If you don't marry him, I will.'

'What a wonderful feeling to be wanted. Did she tell you

about the Japanese twins?'

'Yes she did,' punching him on the arm, 'but it's not going to be like that.'

'Have you got a coin? I need to toss up.'

'What about?'

'Now that there is two of you I have to decide which one.'

'You can't do that; you've already asked me.'

'Yes, but...you didn't really answer me but just kissed me. You didn't say or sign anything.'

He flung his arms around her and said, 'Now you have learned something about me. I tease people too much. I'm sorry, this is too important to joke about. I do love you and I want to marry you and only you. But I'm also pleased that I get a nice mother-in-law because that means when you get older, you'll be just like her.'

Someone coughed and said, 'Excuse me.' They broke apart and Miss Langlang from the agency was standing beside them. She held a fat envelope saying, 'Here's some more stories for you. My friend Dr Lourdes has written them out. She's a good writer because she is a doctor of English literature.

Joe put the envelope aside saying, 'I don't feel like reading about other people's worries just now, I've got enough of my own.'

'Hey, what do you mean, worries?'

Well, I suppose not worries exactly.'

He looked at her fondly, 'My worries have turned into something wonderful.'

The following piece appears on the internet in many places but it's not been possible to contact the writer.

Monday, August 16, 2010

A Day without Filipinos

Let's imagine not just California, but the entire world, waking up one day to discover Filipinos have disappeared. I'm talking here about the six or seven million Filipinos currently working overseas in countries with names that run through the entire alphabet from Angola to Zimbabwe. Let's not worry first about why or how the Filipinos disappeared; in fact, it becomes academic whether it's a day or a week. Just imagine a world without Filipinos.

Think of all the homes dependent on Filipino housekeepers, nannies and caregivers. Those homes would be chaotic as kids cry out for their nannies. Hong Kong and Singaporean and Taiwanese yuppie couples are now forced to stay home realizing, goodness, there's so much of housework that has to be done, how demanding their kids can be and hey, what's this strange language they're babbling in?

It's not just the children that are affected. The problems are even more serious with the elderly in homes and nursing institutions, because Filipino caregivers have provided so much of the critical services they need. When temporary contractual workers are brought in from among non-Filipinos, the elderly complain. They want their Filipino caregivers back because they have that special touch, that extra patience and willingness to stay an hour more when needed.

Hospitals, too, are adversely affected because so many of the disappeared Filipinos were physicians, nurses and other health professionals. All appointments for rehabilitation services, from children with speech problems to stroke survivors, are indefinitely postponed because of disappeared speech pathologists, occupational and physical therapists!

Eventually, the hospital administrators announce they won't take in any more patients unless their conditions are serious. Patients are told to follow their doctors' written orders and, if they have questions, to seek advice on several Internet medical sites. But within two days, the hospitals are swamped with new complaints. The web sites aren't working because of missing Filipino web designers and web site managers.

Service establishments throughout the world—restaurants, supermarkets, hotels—all close down because of their missing key staff involved in management and maintenance. In Asia, hotels complain about the missing bands and singers.

In the United States, many commercial establishments have to close shop, not just because of the missing Filipino sales staff but because their suppliers have all been sending in notices about delays in shipments. Yup, the shipping industry has gone into a crisis too because of missing Filipino seafarers.

Shipping firms begin to look into the emergency recruitment of non-Filipino seafarers but then declare another crisis: They're running out of supplies of oil for their ships because the Middle Eastern countries have come to a standstill without their Filipino workers, including quite a few working for the oil industry.

Frantic presidents and prime ministers call on the United Nations to convene a special session of the Security Council, but the Secretary General says he can't do that with the UN system itself on the edge, with so many of their secretarial and clerical staff, as well as translators, who have disappeared from their main headquarters in

New York and Geneva, as well as their regional offices throughout the world. Quite a number of UN services, especially refugee camps, are also in danger of closing down because of missing Filipino health professionals and teachers.

The Secretary General also explains that he can't convene UN meetings because the airports in New York, Washington and other major US cities have been shut down. The reason? The disappeared Filipinos included quite a few airport security personnel who used to check passengers and their baggage.

The Sec Gen calls on the World Bank and international private foundations for assistance but they're crippled, too, because their Filipino consultants and staff are nowhere to be seen. Funds can't be remitted and projects can't run without the technical assistance provided for by Filipinos.

An exasperated UN Secretary General calls on religious leaders to pray, and pray hard. But when he phones the Pope, he is told the Catholic Church, too, is in crisis because the disappeared include the many Filipino priests and nuns in Rome who help run day-to-day activities, as well as missionaries in the front lines of remote posts, often the only ones providing basic social services.

As they converse, Pope and the Sec Gen agree on one thing: the world has become a quieter place since the Filipinos disappeared. It isn't just the silencing of work and office equipment formerly handled by Filipinos; no, it seems there's much less laughter now that the Filipinos aren't around, the laughter not only of the Filipinos but those they served.

I know, I know, I'm exaggerating the contributions of Filipinos to the world but I'm doing what the producers of 'A Day without Mexicans' had in mind: using a bit of hyperbole to shake people up.

The blurb for their film goes: 'How do you make the invisible, visible? Make them invisible.'

As I wrote this column, I did realize I was doing this not so much for the Hong Kong Chinese and Taiwanese and Singaporeans and Americans who don't appreciate us enough, than, for us Filipinos are pretty good at putting ourselves down, at making ourselves invisible. - Fr. Jess E. Briones, SVD, INQUIRER.net, Posted date: May 29, 2007

A Day without a Filipino

Muhammad Al-Maghrabi became handicapped and shut down his flower and gifts shop business in Jeddah after his Filipino workers insisted on leaving and returning home. He says: 'When they left, I felt as if I had lost my arms. I was so sad that I lost my appetite.'

Al-Maghrabi then flew to Manila to look for two other Filipino workers to replace the ones who had left. Previously, he had tried workers of different nationalities but they did not impress him. 'There is no comparison between Filipinos and others,' he says. Whenever I see Filipinos working in the Kingdom, I wonder what our life would be without them.

Saudi Arabia has the largest number of Filipino workers - 1,019,577 - outside the Philippines. In 2006 alone, the Kingdom recruited more than 223,000 workers from the Philippines and their numbers are still increasing. Filipinos not only play an important and effective role in the Kingdom, they also perform different jobs in countries across the world, including working as sailors. They are known for their professionalism and the quality of their work.

Nobody here can think of a life without Filipinos, who make up around 20 percent of the world's seafarers. There are 1.2 million Filipino sailors.

So if Filipinos decided one day to stop working or go on strike for any reason, who would transport oil, food and heavy equipment across the world? We can only imagine the disaster that would happen.

What makes Filipinos unique is their ability to speak very good English and the technical training they receive in the early stages of their education. There are several specialized training institutes in the Philippines, including those specializing in engineering and road maintenance. This training background makes them highly competent in these vital areas.

When speaking about the Philippines, we should not forget Filipino nurses. They are some 23 percent of the world's total number of nurses. The Philippines is home to over 190 accredited nursing colleges and institutes, from which some 9,000 nurses graduate each year. Many of them work abroad in countries such as the US, the UK, Saudi Arabia, the United Arab Emirates, Kuwait and Singapore.

Cathy Ann, a 35-year-old Filipina nurse who has been working in the Kingdom for the last five years and before that in Singapore, said she does not feel homesick abroad because 'I am surrounded by my compatriots everywhere.' Ann thinks that early training allows Filipinos to excel in nursing and other vocations. She started learning this profession at the age of four as her aunt, a nurse, used to take her to hospital and ask her to watch the work. 'She used to kiss me whenever I learned a new thing. At the age of 11, I could do a lot. I began doing things like measuring my grandfather's blood pressure and giving my mother her insulin injections,' she said.

This type of early education system is lacking in the Kingdom. Many of our children reach the university stage without learning anything except boredom.

The Philippines, which you can barely see on the map, is a very effective country thanks to its people. It has the ability to influence the entire world economy.

We should pay respect to Filipino workers, not only by employing them but also by learning from their valuable experiences.

We should learn and educate our children on how to operate and maintain ships and oil tankers, as well as planning and nursing and how to achieve perfection in our work. This is a must so that we do not become like Muhammad Al-Maghrabi who lost his interest and appetite when Filipino workers left his flower shop.

We have to remember that we are very much dependent on the Filipinos around us. We could die a slow death if they chose to leave us.

From: Arab News -- 7/11/2008

ACKNOWLEDGEMENTS

My thanks to the following people who shared their stories. Names within the stories have been changed where requested.

Tessa Mijares
Louie Bernado
Rose Guangan
Alberta Jomanyn
Juvenlene Altisa
Danilyn Coquong
Adelita Balaba
Jeana Aguila Tengco
Analisa Angie Isaw
Roselyn Laguna
Leordes Bersano
Nova Kubai
Teresa Samiento
Maria Pontonila
Lily Sunico
Pacita Ronda
Grecio Contado
Maria Cabagte
Ruby Ann Lamoste
Nelda Quilaton
Lilibeth Luna
Salome Ignacio
Candalaria Raritna
Ina Vallenuva
Sandra Ardnajela
Enrico Wong
Joy Garci
Olanda Rodrigus
Edna Roks
Arlene

www.ingramcontent.com/pod-product-compliance
Lightning Source LLC
Chambersburg PA
CBHW070722240426
43673CB00003B/113